# Arab, Armenian, Syrian, Lebanese, East Indian, Pakistani and Bangla Deshi Americans: A Study Guide and Source Book

## Kananur V. Chandras

San Francisco, California
1977

Published by
R&E Research Associates , Inc.
4843 Mission Street
San Francisco, California  94112
Publishers
Robert D. Reed and Adam S. Eterovich

Library of Congress Card Catalog Number

77-081032

I.S.B.N.

0-88247-475-8

Dedication

To my children Tara, Kiran and Sunil who made my job enjoyable.

## ACKNOWLEDGMENTS

I am greatly indebted to Ms. Wilma Anderson, Reference Librarian at The Hunt Memorial Library, Fort Valley State College, for her generous assistance in obtaining material from other libraries.

I am grateful to my wife Janet S. Chandras, for her kind cooperation and understanding in making this publication possible.

I thank the editor and publisher of R&E Research Associates, for giving me this opportunity to contribute on Arab Americans, Armenian Americans, Syrian Americans, Lebanese Americans, and East Indian, Pakistani and Bangla Deshi Americans.


Fort Valley, Georgia

1977                                    Kananur V. Chandras, Ph.D.

# TABLE OF CONTENTS

Dedication . . . . . . . . . . . . . . . . . . . . . . . . . . . . . . . .   iii

Acknowledgments. . . . . . . . . . . . . . . . . . . . . . . . . . . . .   v

Introduction . . . . . . . . . . . . . . . . . . . . . . . . . . . . . .   ix

Arab Americans . . . . . . . . . . . . . . . . . . . . . . . . . . . .   1

    Part I:  Arab American Identity . . . . . . . . . . . . . . . . .   1

    Part II:  Arab-American Conflict. . . . . . . . . . . . . . . . .   18

    Part III:  Integration vs. Nationalism
    Arab American Dilemma . . . . . . . . . . . . . . . . . . . . . .   22

    Arab American Bibliography. . . . . . . . . . . . . . . . . . . .   30

Armenian Americans . . . . . . . . . . . . . . . . . . . . . . . . .   32

    Part I:  Armenian American Identity . . . . . . . . . . . . . .   32

    Part II:  Armenian American Conflict. . . . . . . . . . . . . .   46

    Part III:  Integration versus Nationalism
    Armenian American Dilemma . . . . . . . . . . . . . . . . . . .   49

    Armenian American Bibliography. . . . . . . . . . . . . . . . .   53

Middle Eastern Americans . . . . . . . . . . . . . . . . . . . . . .   54

    Part I:  Middle Eastern American Identity . . . . . . . . . . .   54

    Part II:  Syrian and Lebanese Americans' Conflict . . . . . .   66

    Part III:  Integration versus Nationalism
    Middle Eastern American Dilemma . . . . . . . . . . . . . . . .   68

    Middle Eastern-American Bibliography. . . . . . . . . . . . . .   71

East Indian, Pakistani and Bangla Deshi Americans. . . . . . . . .   73

    Part I:  East Indian, Pakistani and Bangla Deshi
    Americans' Identity. . . . . . . . . . . . . . . . . . . . . . .   73

    Part II:  East Indian, Pakistani and Bangla Deshi
    Americans' Conflict. . . . . . . . . . . . . . . . . . . . . . .   96

    Part III:  Integration versus Nationalism
    East Indian, Pakistani and Bangla Deshi
    Americans' Dilemma. . . . . . . . . . . . . . . . . . . . . . .   113

    East Indian, Pakistani and Bangla Deshi Americans'
    Bibliography. . . . . . . . . . . . . . . . . . . . . . . . . .   118

# INTRODUCTION

During the past few years, it has become increasingly clear to American public and scholars alike that some neglected minority groups have become important
for study and research. In this book four American minority groups are studied
under three themes: Identity, Conflict, and Integration/Nationalism. This book
serves as a text or course guide for the student or teacher in the study of four
minority groups--Arab Americans, Armenian Americans, Syrian Americans, Lebanese
Americans, East Indian, Pakistani and Bangla Deshi Americans.

This book examines the problems minority groups have faced (and continue to
face) in the United States. Some of the other topics discussed in the book are:
the reasons for immigration, problems faced by the minority groups or group members
in the United States, the contributions of the group members to the American
society and culture, and the present status of minority groups in the United
States.

The study outline is historical and chronological in development. It provides the reader with rich and valuable information by using multidisciplinary
approach.

The "Notes and Sources" column provides references to the material presented
in the study outline. At times notes are provided in the column to elaborate or
expand upon the study outline.

PART I:  ARAB AMERICAN IDENTITY

I.  Introduction

The primary emphasis in this part is on the Arab-American immigrants who came to the United States from Egypt, Jordan, Syria, Lebanon, Iraq, Saudi Arabia, Sudan, Algeria, Morocco, and Tunisia, as well as a number of small predominantly Muslim nations in the Mid-East.  According to the United States Census, there were approximately 1.66 million Arab-Americans in the U.S. in 1970.  Recently, their numbers have increased greatly.

Arab immigrants brought with them to America a rich and proud history.  In past centuries they built great centers of civilization and learning, and made brilliant contributions in the arts and sciences when Europe was in the "Dark Ages."

As a group, immigrants from Arab countries may be characterized as absorbing American values and social structures while retaining their other identities as bases for relating to each other.

Many aspects of Arab philosophy, tradition and custom had made it easy for the immigrants to acculturate to the host culture.  Arab values such as hard work, discipline, and ethics, were similar to those of American values.

As an ethnic community, Arab-Americans have distinguished themselves in many ways, in the pluralistic American society.

II.  Guide and Sourcebook

| *Study Outline* | *Notes and Sources* |
|---|---|
| A.  Arab immigrants who came to the United States had a long and proud history. | Philip K. Hitti, History of the Arabs, 10th edition, London:  Macmillan, 1970. |
| 1.  Arab civilization made brilliant contributions to the world culture. | (By 2700 B.C. there had emerged in Egypt a Civilization with a strong centralized government, a complex form of writing as well as the paper and ink with which to write, a distinctive and monumental art form, the beginnings of scientific medical |

1

| Study Outline | Notes and Sources |
|---|---|

diagnoses, and the first calendar of 365 days.)

Margaret Gillett, A History of Education, New York: McGraw-Hill Co. of Canada Ltd., 1966, p. 13.

(Arabs translated and preserved Greco-Roman educational and scientific books. In the 12th century Europeans started opening schools to translate the works of the Arabs in philosophy, medicine, chemistry, history, astrology, and other subjects.)

a) Arabs were responsible for transmitting Greek and Roman Civilization to Europe.

b) Arab medicine and curricula dominated the European schools until the 17th century.

c) One of the most important contributions of the Arabs to Western Civilization was their transmittal of the numerals, the zero, and the decimal systems.

(Al-Khwarizmi was the first Arab exponent of the use of numerals, including zero, in preference to letters. These numerals he called Hinki, indicating their Indian origin.)

d) Arabs made great advances in astronomy.

(The leading Arab astronomers were Al Battani (858-929 A.D.) Al Biruni (973-1048 A.D.). They also discussed the possibility of the earth's rotation around its axis, 500 years before Galileo.)

| | |
|---|---|
| *Study Outline* | *Notes and Sources* |

e) The Arab contribution to the study of Geography was immense. They kept alive the ancient doctrine of the sphericity of the earth, without which the discovery of the New World would not have been possible.

(The pioneer in Geography was the great traveler, Ibn-Bat-Tuta. Arabs reached India, Indonesia, Malaysia, and the Phillipines, where they spread their civilization, religion, and trade.)

f) Arabs used the most advanced astronomical and navigational instruments that were available to any country.

(When Vasco da Gama reached Africa, he could not move any further without the help of his Arab pilot, Ahmad-Ibn-Majid, who possessed the maps and navigation instruments necessary to cross the Indian Ocean to Calicut. This opened the road to western navigation.)

g) Arabs advanced the frontiers of science and invented machines.

  (1) Al Kindi wrote on specific weights, optics, light reflection and tide.

  (2) Among the Arab developments were clocks run by mercury, or by burning candles.

  (3) Arabs in the 13th century were

the first to use a magnetic
compass for navigation.

(4) Ibn-al-Haytham (965 A.D.) wrote
a book, Kitab Al Manazir, which
contained a wealth of scientific
knowledge unknown to the West.

(His book influenced the scientific
thought for six to seven centuries.
He dealt the following areas:
optical illusions, the structure of
the eye, comets and mirages.)

(5) Some of the other inventions
were in hydraulics.

h) Arab art, pottery, painting,
sculpture and architecture were
an indisputable proof of their
achievement in the world long before America became a nation.

Ernst Kuhnel, The Minor Arts of
Islam, New York:  Cornell University
Press, 1971.

i) In religion and philosophy, Arab
thought has influenced much of
the world.

Bernard Lewis, The Arabs in History,
London:  Hutchinson University
Library, 1966, p. 133.

(1) The majority religion in the
Arab world is Islam.  Islam
means, "submission to the will
of Allah," and "Moslem" means
"one who submits."

(Islam was founded by Arab Prophet
Muhammad, 570-632 A.D.  The Quran
is the holy book of Arab Moslems.

(a) In Islam, there are two main
divisions, the Sunni and the
Shia.

Islam was not only a system of belief
and cult, it was also a system of
state, society, law, thought and art--
a civilization with religion as its
unifying, and eventually dominating,

| Study Outline | Notes and Sources |
|---|---|

factor.)

(2) Another aspect of Islam has been almost equally important for the rank and file of the faithful is Sufism or mysticism, as it is usually translated.

Margaret Smith, Readings from Mystics of Islam, London: Wisdom of the East Series, 1932. (Sufis have been great missionaries of Islam. They influenced people in India, Anatolia, Africa, and Indonesia. They made themselves responsible for the spiritual care of the masses.)

(3) Christianity is a minority religion in the Arab countries.

(Middle Eastern Christendom is divided. There are the Orthodox churches--Greek, Syrian, Armenian, and others. Second, there is the heretical Coptic church, to which majority of Egyptian Christians belong. Third, there are the Uniat churches, which rejoined Roman Catholicism. The Maronite church in Lebanon is the most important Uniat body in the Middle East. Finally, there are a few protestants.

j) The Arab world had a rich tradition of art, music and literature.

Oleg Grabar, The Formation of Islamic Art, New Haven, Connecticut: Yale University Press, 1973.

| Study Outline | Notes and Sources |
|---|---|
| (1) All Arab visual art is decorative, never, only extremely rarely is it representational. | David T. Rice, Islamic Art, New York: Praeger, 1965. (In art, the early Muslims excelled in gold and silver, response and inlay.) |
| (2) Arabic music first started to exert its influence when Byzantium ceased to be the center of the intellectual world. | Henry G. Farmer, Oriental Studies: Mainly Musical, London: Itinrichsen, 1953. (Music is an integral part of the Arab world, an indispensable element in its communal, tribal, and home life.) |
| (3) The highest achievement of the Arabs was in poetry and the allied art of rhetoric. | (The Quran itself was the first document of Arab prose literature.) |
| k) Arab culture also provided a strong sense of identity to Arab-Americans and their American-born children. | |
| B. The history of the Arab-American in the United States is a part of his more immediate cultural heritage, and is evidence of his own American identity. | "Arab-Adventures in the New World," Yearbook, 1965-66, New York: The Action Committee on American Arab Relations, 1966. Also see the article in the same Yearbook, "The Arabs who followed Columbus." |

| Study Outline | Notes and Sources |
|---|---|
| 1. Several factors influenced Arabs to begin immigration to America. | W. Lloyd Warner and Leo Srole, *The Social System of American Ethnic Groups*, New Haven: Yale University Press, 1945, p. 105. |
| a) Deterioration of the Turkish Ottoman Empire and control of Arab lands by the colonial powers (mainly British and French) were some of the reasons. | |
| b) The news of economic opportunities brought many Arabs to America. | (Many young men who had heard that the streets of New York were paved with gold were intent on getting their share and returning to their native villages in the Middle East to enjoy life forever. Contrary to their expectations, American streets were not paved with gold nor did money trees grow wild in the land of economic miracles and opportunities.) |
| c) They came to America to escape economic stagnation and low standards of living for themselves and their families. | |
| d) Social, political and religious discriminations in their native land forced many Arabs to | |

immigrate to the United States.

e) Estephen the Arab (1539 A.D.), a
Moroccan, who was the guide to
Fra de Niza, a Franciscan, came to
explore the northern region of
America and to prepare for the
expedition.

f) The historian Makdisi says that
there were other pioneers who came
to America from Arabic countries,
like Egyptian Nasserdine and the
Wahab families.

(The Wahab family in North Carolina
originally came from Morocco where
they were Wahabists, a movement
similar to puritanism which was
strong in the early eighteenth
century Arab world.)

g) The first Arabic speaking immigrant to set foot in the U.S. was
the Lebanese, Antonious al-
Bishallany in Boston in 1854.

h) In 1856, the first shipment of 33
camels arrived in the U.S. with a
chief cameleer who was a Lebanese
called Hadji Ali, later nicknamed
"Hi Jolly."

i) It was around 1875 when signifi-
cant numbers of Arabic speaking
immigrants started to enter the
United States.

| *Study Outline* | *Notes and Sources* |
|---|---|
| j) The first family to arrive in the United States was that of Joseph Arbeely of Damascus in 1878. | Philip K. Kitti, <u>The Syrians in America</u>, New York: Doran, 1924, p. v. |
| k) The group migration of the Arabs into the United States occurred in four main waves: 1900-1912, 1930-1938, 1947-1960, and 1967 on. | (About 90% of the immigrants and their descendants were Christians from the Lebanese region. During 1900-1938, a quarter of a million Arabs entered the U.S. from greater Syria and Lebanon. Those who came during the third and fourth waves, 1947-1960 and 1967-1976 were for the most part either educated or of at least moderate means financially.) |
| l) The first period of increased migration to the U.S. from 1865 to 1915, was terminated by World War I. | |
| m) The Quota Law which has been implemented since 1924 was a factor in limiting Arab immigration to the U.S. | |
| n) Only after World War II, were the restrictions relaxed. A great proportion of the Arab students who came to study in the U.S. | |

9

| *Study Outline* | *Notes and Sources* |
|---|---|

stayed to work in America after
completing their studies.

o) By 1970, there were more than
1.66 million Arab-Americans in
the United States. A large
number of them were professionals.

Arab American University Graduates,
Newsletter, Vol. VI, No. 5,
December 1973.

2. The Arab-family patterns and traditions influenced (and are still influencing) the home life of Arab-
Americans.

   a) In the beginning, marriages were
   not usually the western style
   love marriages.

Jon C. Swanson, "Mate Selection and
Intermarriage in an American Arab
Moslem Community," Univ. of Iowa,
unpublished M.A. thesis, 1970.
R. P. Davies, "Syrian Arabic Kinship
Terms," Southwestern Journal of
Anthropology, Vol. 3, No. 3 (Autumn
1949), 244-52.

   b) Even today, the Arab Muslims resist inter-religious marriages
   unless the spouse becomes Muslim.

Elaine C. Hagopian and Ann Paden
(ed.), The Arab-Americans, Illinois:
The Medina University Press International, 1969, p. 13.

   c) The Arab Christians do not resist
   inter-ethnic marriage with Americans. Generally, they encourage
   this trend.

| *Study Outline* | *Notes and Sources* |
|---|---|
| d) Activities, friendships and employment were family-centered. (Contemporary activities, friendship and employment are still family-centered.) | (Arab-American families tended to be tight, self-centered, self-sufficient units controlled by parental authority. Family organization followed patterns which in many ways remained unchanged generation after generation.) |
| e) Family life remained strictly patriarchal one generation after another, but motherhood was something almost sacred. | (Also refer to Abdo A. Elkholy, The Arab Moslems in the United States, New Haven: College and University Press, 1966, pp. 28-35. |
| f) Later generations of Arab-Americans found chances for upward mobility improved. | |
| g) In general, Arab-American Moslem young men have adopted a liberal attitude toward inter-religious marriage. | (However, they are still strongly opposed to their women marrying non-Moslems. The second and third generations tend to intermarry with the Americans.) (In contrast to the mixed religious marriage, Arab-Americans are very rigid concerning mixed marriage with blacks.) |
| h) Second and third generation Arab-Americans concerned themselves with education and with entering | Barbara C. Aswad (ed.), Arabic Speaking Communities in American Cities, New York: The Center for |

the professions. More stress had been placed on the professions and education than on maintaining small stores.

Migration Studies of New York, Inc., 1974, pp. 35-36.

(Until the past decade, Arab-Americans found a hospitable climate for small-scale retail grocery stores. That climate has changed considerably since about 1965 when many cities suffered from civil disturbances of major proportions. Many Arab-American businesses and stores were damaged or destroyed. The main factor involved in this situation has been the increased irritation of the predominantly black residents of inner city toward businesses of all kinds, especially non-black businesses in their neighborhoods.)

3. Since late 1967, modest estimates indicate that almost 30,000 Arab intellectuals have left Egypt, Syria, and Iraq for America. And some 70,000 preceded them between 1957 and 1967. The entry of these professionals from the Arab world is increasing every year.

4. The educated, highly professional

Joseph R. Haiek, The American Arabic

| Study Outline | Notes and Sources |
|---|---|

## Study Outline

Arab-Americans occupy prominent
positions in American society.

C. America created its own definitions
of Arab-American identity which have
had varying psychological effects on
Arab-Americans' perceptions of themselves.

1. There were positive stereotypes.

   a) Employees viewed them as good
   and honest laborers.

      (1) Arab-American laborers had a
      strong sense of obligation.

      (2) Many of them earned their way
      through persistence and hard
      work under other Arab-Americans.

      (3) They worked long hours under
      depressing conditions.

      (4) The Arab immigrants were success-
      ful in their economic pursuits.

   b) The Arab-American religions and
   family traditions fit in well with
   American cultural patterns.

      (1) Arab-American children behaved
      well, treating parents and
      elders, and authorities with
      respect.

## Notes and Sources

Speaking Community: 1975 Almanac,
Los Angeles, California: The News
Circle, 1975.

13

(2) Arab-American families were close knit and the members displayed solidarity and a willingness to sacrifice for other members of the family.

Affif I. Tannous, The Arab Village Community in the Middle East, Washington, D.C.:  Smithsonian Institute, 1943, p. 537.

(3) In the patriarchal family, the father was the symbol of authority and the mother gave stability to the home by answering to the physical and emotional needs of the children.

(4) Most Arab-Americans brought with them a strong sense of duty to their community and family.

(5) Arab-American' high priority on hard work and excellence were consistent with American ideals, though such standards often led to conflict--dislike and agitation against them.

Barbara C. Aswad, Arabic Speaking Communities in American Cities, pp. 35-36.
(Arab Americans' economic success often bring resentment from other racial groups in America.)

D.  Many Arab-Americans have made outstanding contributions to their country and to the world in all fields of human endeavor.

1.  Arab-Americans in Science

   - Dr. Mitry P. Ajalat, the first president of the first Arab American Medical

Association in California.

- Dr. Nicholas S. Assali, Professor of Obstetrics.

- Dr. Michael E. DeBakey, Heart Surgeon, a pioneer in Cardio-Vascular disease surgery. He was the first to use a heart pump successfully on a patient.

- Dr. Mostafa Amr El-Sayed, chemist and space technologist.

- Dr. Alexander A. Kirkish, well known dentist.

- Dr. Howard P. Monsour, Surgeon.

- Dr. Robert G. Monsour, specialist in psychiatry and neurology.

- Dr. Roy C. Monsour, medical doctor.

- Dr. William J. Monsour, specialist in cardiology.

- Dr. M. Hadi Salem, well known Thoracic surgeon.

- Dr. Ali Seif, distinguished surgeon.

- Dr. George Doumani, geologist.

- Dr. Farouk El-Baz, space age geologist.

2. <u>In politics, Arab-Americans are beginning to provide leadership</u>

- James Abourezk, U.S. Senator from South Dakota

- Abraham Kazen, U.S. Congressman from Texas

- Jim Abdnor, U.S. Congressman from Nebraska

- Toby Moffett, U.S. Congressman from Connecticut

- James R. Deeb, State Senator in Florida

- Thomas L. Hazouri, State Congressman in Florida

- Edward Hanna, Mayor of Utica, New York

- James J. Tayoun, State Congressman in Pennsylvania

- Victor Atiyeh, Oregon State Senator

- George Kasem, Oregon State House of Representative

3. Scholars

   - Ayad Sayid Ali Al-Qazzaz, sociologist specializing in political and military sociology of the Middle East.

   - Matti Moosa, Professor of History and Cultures of Middle East

   - Clement J. Nouri, Educator, Dean, School of Business Administration, University of San Diego

   - Butros Abdal-Malik, Professor of History

   - Anwar G. Chejne, Professor of Arabic

   - Samir K. Hamarneh, Curator-Historian, Smithsonian Institute

4. Entertainment, Broadcasting

   - Sadik E. Adlai, President of Cinema Artists in Hollywood

   - William J. Baroody, President, American Enterprise Institute

   - George Oliver Cory, Broadcast Executive

   - Jamie Farr, Actor

   - Edmonde Alex Haddad, Radio Commentator

   - Hassan I. Husseini, Journalist, broadcaster

   - Mardi Rustam, Movie producer, actor, president of International Film Lab. Inc.

   - Fouad Said, Movie Producer

5. Enterpreneurs, Businessmen

   - Khalil A. Ali, Founder of Alfa Auto Rentals and Leasing in Beverly Hills

   - Earnest George, Businessman

   - Minor George, Enterpreneur

   - Dan Hanna, Portland Enterpreneur

   - Tawfiq N. Khoury, Real Estate Broker

   - Mansour H. Laham, Pioneer manufacturer in plastic, rubber and allied

16

chemical materials

- George Maloof, Real Estate Broker

- Frank Maria, Management consultant

- Elia Najar, businessman

- John Shaheen, enterpreneur

- Thelma Shain, enterpreneur

- Nicholas Shammas, enterpreneur

- Anthony Abraham, owner of one of the world's largest retail automobile

  dealerships

- Robert S. Andrews, enterpreneur

- B. D. Eddie, businessman

- Raymond Jallow, chief economist and enterpreneur

- Norman N. Mamey, enterpreneur

- Frank E. Swyden, businessman

- Woodrow W. Woody, enterpreneur

- Harry Zachary, enterpreneur

6. Writers

- William Peter Blatty, author of best selling books

- Helen E. Corey, author of a best seller

- Samuel Hazo, professor, poet and writer

- Labeebee J. H. Saquet, writer

PART II: ARAB-AMERICAN CONFLICT

I.  Introduction

The Arab immigrants and their children had the usual cultural and linguistic
conflicts to deal with in the United States.  The early immigrants encountered
hard economic conditions and earned their way through persistence and hard work as
farmers, storekeepers, and laborers.  Many were successful in establishing themselves as politicians, businessmen, entrepreneurs and professionals.  This was
striking, especially in light of the low educational level of those early immigrants.

In the absence of any physical or racial distinction to reveal their Middle
Eastern origin, the second and third generations found themselves fully accepted
by the American society.

II.  Guide and Sourcebook

| *Study Outline* | *Notes and Sources* |
|---|---|
| A.  It was a type of conflict--the strug-gle to make the greatest amount of money in the shortest possible period of time and also to escape the mili-tary oppression and religious perse-cution--which brought the Arab immi-grant to America, where he thought to find means to better conditions for his immediate family and extended family. | (A majority of the Christian Arabs have migrated to the United States in the past half century.  Immigra-tion to the United States became attractive because here the environ-ment seemed to have evolved a temper which permits a tolerance of cultural pluralism, a tolerance which promises hopes for the continued integrity of the community and its cultural heri-tage.  Another reason was to escape their minority status as Christians in the changing Arab world.  Arab Christians in America still outnumber Arab Muslims by a ratio of nine to one.) |

18

| Study Outline | Notes and Sources |
|---|---|

Study Outline

1. Many Arab Americans intended to make greatest possible amount of money and return to their homeland.

2. To find religious freedom and to escape religious persecution at home they emigrated to America.

3. Many Arab immigrants left their homeland to escape political oppression.

4. The Arab world was faced with the problem of overpopulation.

B. The Arab immigrants who landed in America encountered hard economic conditions but earned their way through persistence and hard work as farmers, peddlers, storekeepers, and laborers.

1. Majority of the immigrants, Muslim and Christian alike, came neither from the elite nor the sharecropping classes, but from towns or villages in the rural areas where most owned property. Some were small merchants.

2. After their arrival in America, the economically oriented Arab immigrants became merchants, white

Notes and Sources

(Arab-American Christians still remember the 1860 massacre of Christians by the Muslims in the Middle East.

Abdo A. Elkholy, "The Arab-Americans: Nationalism and Traditional Preservations," in The Arab Americans, edited by Elaine C. Hagopian and Ann Paden, p. 7.

Mary C. Sengstock, "Iraqi Christians in Detroit: An Analysis of Ethnic Occupation," in Arabic Speaking

19

| Study Outline | Notes and Sources |
|---|---|

collar workers and professionals.

3. Some of them opened grocery stores,
   restaurants, bars, and other
   businesses which helped the Arab-
   American family to exceed the
   average income of all American
   families in this period.

C. Practices within the Arab-American
   community led to personal or group
   conflicts.

1. Sometimes tensions between Christian
   and Muslim Arab immigrants and
   among their own groups, were very
   high.

2. Many Arab immigrants felt anxiety
   and alienation in overcrowded
   settlements where landlords rented
   sleeping space to as many as the
   floors would accommodate.

3. Several families occupied the same
   flats and shared kitchen and other
   facilities.

Communities in American Cities, by
Barbara C. Aswad (ed.), New York:
The Center for Migration Studies,
1974, pp. 21-36.
Abdo A. Elkholy, The Arab Moslems
in the United States, Connecticut:
College and University Press, 1960,
pp. 17-18.

(In 1909, there was violence in
Springfield, Massachusetts, between
Muslim and Christian Arab immigrants.
Arab Americans still identify them-
selves as Lebanese, Syrian, Iraqi,
etc.)

(Some of these reasons may have contributed to the tensions among the
Arab immigrant community.)

| Study Outline | Notes and Sources |
|---|---|

4. The streets where the Arab immigrants lived were dirty and unpaved.

D. The immigration laws and the world conditions curtailed the number of Arab immigrants to the United States.

1. The period of increased Arab immigration to the United States was between 1865 and 1915.

(Larger steamships handled increased passenger trade from the Arab countries.)

2. Later immigrations were terminated by the coming of World War I.

3. The immigration law of 1924, assigned a small quota for Arab countries.

4. After the end of World War II, the restrictions on Arab immigration were relaxed.

5. The passage of the Immigration and Naturalization Act of 1965, relaxed the immigration restrictions of Arabs by abolishing the quota system.

(The fifth immigration preference created by the Immigration Law helped many Arab-American citizens to bring to the States, as immigrants, their immediate relatives. For an educated or skilled Arab could acquire permanent status in the U.S. within three months, off quota.

PART III:  INTEGRATION VS. NATIONALISM
ARAB-AMERICAN DILEMMA

I.    Introduction

Most Arab-immigrants from the Arab world had strong nationalistic sentiments.
They maintained cultural and family ties in the Middle East and also supported parents, families and relatives in the old country.  They hoped to return to the old
country once they had earned enough money to retire.

First generation Arab immigrants shared a common historical and cultural heritage (especially the Arabic language).  However, there were numerous subgroups
(Muslims, Christians and others) within this broad category of peoples and the
immigrants did not reflect all the social groupings in the Arab world.  They formed
ethnic enclaves for the sake of survival in the alien culture.

Later generations did not acquire strong cultural ties with the countries of
their parents.  Elkholy in his book, The Arab Americans states that "20% of the
second generation and 71% of the third generation neither understood nor read
Arabic."  It is of interest to note that the sense of Arab nationalism was found
to be higher in the third Arab-Muslim generation in some Arab communities in the
United States than in the marginal second generation.

A number of organizations of the American Arabic speaking community in the
United States developed to represent aspects of the contrasting impulses to
nationalism or integration.  Some of the organizations are listed in the notes
and sources.

The creation of Israel as a homeland for the Jewish people intensified
nationalistic feelings among the Arab-Americans.  Throughout the last three
decades, the Arab countries have been in a state of war against Israel.  The defeat of Arab armies by the Israelis aroused anger and shame among the Arab-American
Muslims.  This in turn, heightened nationalism.

The present status of Arab-Americans lies somewhere between the poles of
nationalism and integration.  The second and third generation of Arab-Americans
have adopted the middle class cultural values of America, but still they are part
of a pluralistic American society which is closer to pluralism than to complete
integration.

II.   Guide and Sourcebook

                    *Study Outline*                                    *Notes and Sources*

A.  The relations of the Arab immigrants

    in America with the old countries were

    very strong.  They maintained their

    cultural identity and the intention of

22

returning to their homeland to buy a
few acres, build modest homes, get
married, and settle down.

1.  The early Arab immigrants found it
    almost imperative to congregate in
    physical proximity for the sake of
    survival in the American culture.

2.  Faced with the language barrier,
    early Arab immigrants found it
    natural to form their own small
    communities.

3.  Loyalty of Arab-Americans to their
    families was reflected in their
    financial support of families and
    community institutions.

    Elaine C. Hagopian, "The Institutional
    Development of the Arab-American
    Community in Boston," in The Arab
    Americans by Elaine C. Hagopian and
    Ann Paden (ed.), p. 69.

4.  Many Arab-Americans still maintain
    close ties with the homeland by
    observing the religious and cul-
    tural traditions of the old country.

    (The Arab-American community religiously
    belongs to various denominations of
    two religions; Christianity and Islam.
    Most of the pioneering immigrants were
    Christians who followed a number of
    Eastern rite denominations, mainly,
    Antiochian, Orthodox, Maronites,
    Melkites, Copts, Syrians, Assyrians,
    and Chaldeans.  Each denomination is
    grouped around its church, and these

| *Study Outline* | *Notes and Sources* |
|---|---|

can be found in all the major cities of the United States.

B.  The United States' national policies and the conflicts in the Middle East intensified nationalistic feelings of Arab-Americans.

  1.  The Arab-Americans feel a common cultural, religious, and linguistic bond with the Arab countries.

  (Mosques and Islamic centers are to be found throughout the United States.

  2.  For Arab-American Muslims, Gamal Abdel-Nasser became the symbol of Arab nationalism.

  (Nasser came to power in 1952. He was elected President in 1956 and nationalized the Suez Canal the same year.)

  3.  The Middle East conflict has aroused strong nationalistic feelings especially among the Muslim Arab-Americans.

  4.  In the eyes of Arab-American Muslims, the United States' Mideast foreign policy has been less than admirable.

  (The United States commitment to Israel remains unwavering. No American Administration has seriously considered weakening it since its inception in May 1948, when the United States under President Harry S. Truman was the first government to recognize the newly independent Jewish state.

| Study Outline | Notes and Sources |
|---|---|
| | However, increasing dependency on Arab oil is weakening the commitment.) |
| 5. Since the creation of Israel in 1948, the United States heavily supported Israel which alienated many Arab-American Muslims. | (Israel is the only Middle East society that most nearly shares American values of political democracy and Judeo-Christian traditions.) |
| 6. The Israelis gained decisive victories in the first three wars with the Arabs in 1948, 1956, and again in 1967. This aroused the anger of Muslims in America but discouraged them as well. | (In 1973, however, the Arab armies made a better showing in the war against Israel.) |
| 7. Another factor responsible for Arab-American nationalism is the continued and increased connections between the communities in the U.S. and those in the Middle East. | (This may be due to the introduction of Palestinian refugees and immigrants from the Middle East.) |
| 8. The aviation technology has helped Arab-American nationalism through inexpensive air flights to the Arab countries. Thus communications are strengthened, old relationships reestablished and new ones created. | |
| 9. The Arab-American organizations | (Action Committee on American-Arab |

maintained the nationalistic leadership of the Arab-American communities
in the United States.

Relations (ACAAR) was founded in
1964 to foster Arab American understanding and to defend Palestinian
rights.  It has 29 chapters with
about 50,000 members.

Some of the other organizations are:

American Arab Society

American Arab Association

American Ramallah Federation

Arab Physical Society

The Association of Arab-American

  University Graduates (AAUG)

International Arab Federation

United Holy Land Fund

United American Arab Congress

United Arab Community Club

Organization of Arab States and

many others.

10. Arab-American language publications
    promote Arab nationalism.  (There
    were more than 25 Arab-American
    newspapers in 1975.)

Joseph R. Haiek, The American Arabic
Speaking Community, Ca.:  The News
Circle, 1975, pp. 52-58.

11. There are a number of other evidences
    of a cultural separatism which might
    contribute to nationalistic feelings
    such as mosques, Arabic language

(There are over 32 Muslim Mosques
in the United States.)

newspapers and social clubs.

C. American-born Arab-Americans, especially the Arab-American Christians do not accept the separatism of Arab-American community.

D. The nationalism of the Arab-American community in the United States revived after the creation of Israel in 1948, and the consequent displacement of most Palestinians.

1. It is ironical that many self-exiled Arab elites from the Middle East possess bitter feelings towards their homeland. They sympathize with the Arab masses and hope that some day they could unite the Arab countries and liberate them from military domination and corruption.

2. Many Arab-Americans feel that a responsibility of the future is for the Arab countries to liberate Palestine.

(For much of the past 25 to 30 years, the Middle East has been in turmoil. Some Arab countries have been torn by revolution; others have overthrown corrupt governments. Political figures have been targets of assasins. As recently as 1975, King Faisal of Saudi Arabia was gunned down in his own palace.)

(The Arab-Israeli conflict which centers on demands for the return of Arab land occupied by Israel and the return of the Palestinians who left the territory originally designated as Israel, has had worldwide consequences. Arab guerrilla groups have

committed acts of terrorism in all
parts of the world.)

3. The Arab-American groups feel that
   the national policies of the U.S.
   are a good deal more favorably in-
   clined toward Israel than towards
   the Arab nations.

4. The Arab-American political groups
   and other groups have formed to express concern about American
   national policies.

5. The most important factor in awaken-
   ing the Arab-American is the 1967
   defeat of the Arab armies by Israel.
   This incident alienated the Arab-
   Americans to such a degree that
   some of them were willing to join
   forces with Arab nations.

6. Since the 1973 October war with
   Israel in which the Egyptian forces
   destroyed the Bar-Lev line, the
   enthusiasm of the Arab-Americans
   has declined.

7. A number of Arab-American organiza-    (At present, the National Association
   tions and young writers are still       of Arab-Americans and the organization
   promoting Arab-American nationalism.    of Arab-American University Graduates

are the most important Arab-American

organizations which serve as uniting

force among Arab-Americans.)

## Conclusion

Arab immigrants came to America from Egypt, Jordan, Syria, Lebanon, Iraq, Saudi Arabia, Sudan, Algeria, Morocco, Tunisia and other small predominantly Muslim countries in the Middle East. They brought with them a rich and proud history. They came to America to find economic opportunities and to escape social, political and religious discriminations in their native lands.

Arab-Americans like many other immigrant groups in America maintained their cultural identity. But, later generations of Arab-Americans have not strongly identified themselves with past traditions and customs. Many have detached themselves from the cultural practices of their parents and grand parents. They want full participation in the American society.

Many Arab-Americans have made outstanding contributions to America and to the world in all fields of human endeavor.

Today, many Arab-Americans call for a new nationalism based on stronger ties with the Middle Eastern Muslim nations. They feel that the United States should side with Arab countries to liberate Palestine from Israeli occupation.

# BIBLIOGRAPHY

Arab American University Graduates, Newsletter, Vol. VI, No. 5, December 1973.

Aswad, Barbara C. Arabic Speaking Communities in American Cities. New York: The Center for Migration Studies, 1974.

Davies, R. P. "Syrian Arabic Kinship Terms." Southwestern Journal of Anthropology, Vol. 3, No. 3 (Autumn 1949).

Elkholy, Abdo A. "The Arab-Americans: Nationalism and Traditional Preservations." In The Arab Americans by Elaine C. Hagopian and Ann Paden, ed. Illinois: The Medina University Press International, 1969.

Elkholy, Abdo A. The Arab Moslems in the United States. Connecticut: College and University Press, 1960.

Farmer, Henry G. Oriental Studies: Mainly Musical. London: Itinrichsen, 1953.

Gillett, Margaret. A History of Education. New York: McGraw-Hill Co. of Canada Ltd., 1966.

Grabar, Oleg. The Formation of Islamic Art. New Haven, Connecticut: Yale University Press, 1973.

Hagopian, Elaine C. "The Institutional Development of the Arab-American Community in Boston." In The Arab Americans by Elaine C. Hagopian and Ann Paden, ed. Illinois: The Medina University Press International, 1969.

Haiek, Joseph R. The American Arabic Speaking Community. California: The News Circle, 1975.

Kitti, Philip K. The Syrians in America. New York: Doran, 1924.

Kuhnel, Ernst. The Minor Arts of Islam. New York: Cornell University Press, 1971.

Lewis, Bernard. The Arabs in History. London: Hutchinson University Library, 1966.

Rice, David T. Islamic Art. New York: Praeger, 1965.

Sengstock, Mary C. "Iraqi Christians in Detroit: An Analysis of Ethnic Occupation." In Arabic Speaking Communities in American Cities by Barbara C. Aswad, ed. New York: The Center for Migration Studies, 1974.

Smith, Margaret. Readings from Mystics of Islam. London: Wisdom of the East Series, 1932.

Swanson, Jon C. "Mate Selection and Intermarriage in an American Arab Moslem Community." Unpublished M.A. Thesis, University of Iowa, 1970.

Tannous, Affif I. The Arab Village Community in the Middle East. Washington, D.C.: Smithsonian Institute, 1943.

Warner, W. Lloyd, and Srole, Leo. The Social System of American Ethnic Groups.
New Haven, Connecticut: Yale University Press, 1945.

Yearbook, "Arab-Adventures in the New World," 1965-66. New York: The Action
Committee on American Arab Relations, 1966.

I.  Introduction

This part of the book deals with Armenian immigrants and their descendents
in the United States.  Armenian immigrants came from all over the world in search
of freedom, security and economic prosperity.

Armenian immigrants who came to the United States brought with them rich ancient
cultures.  They contributed immensely to the progress of America:  in philosophy
and religion, in literature and the arts, in scientific and technological discoveries
and inventions and in traditions and habits.

Armenian-Americans, like other immigrant groups, sought to retain their cultural identity and maintain family ties; but, American immigration laws made it difficult for them to maintain these ties on a personal basis.  However, in spite of
insurmountable problems in American society they distinguished themselves in all
walks of life:  politics, business, education, military science, and science and
technology.  They made America their home and developed strong loyalties to it.


II.  Guide and Sourcebook

| *Study Outline* | *Notes and Sources* |
|---|---|
| A. Armenian-Americans who settled in the United States were products of rich ancient cultures. | David Marshall Long, Armenia:  Cradle of Civilization, London:  George Allen and Unwin, Ltd., 1970, p. 9. |
| 1. Armenian Civilization has enriched the civilized world through its contributions. | |
| a) Armenians were responsible for many discoveries and inventions which led to technological progress. | |
| (1) Armenians claim their 5,000 year old development of metal- lurgical techniques to be the world's first. | |

32

| Study Outline | Notes and Sources |
|---|---|

<table>
<tr>
<td>

(2) They developed techniques of grinding and polishing for tool making.

(3) They contributed to the world culture in the fields of sewing, weaving and textile manufacture.

</td>
<td>

(Tool making became more specialized and formed the basis of a regular export industry.)

</td>
</tr>
<tr>
<td>

b) Armenian architecture, sculpture, painting, art and pottery influenced many world cultures.

</td>
<td>

J. Arnott Hamilton, Byzantine Architecture and Decoration, London, 1935. Joseph Strzygowski, Origin of Christian Church Art, Oxford, England: 1923. Sakisian Armenag, "Notes on the Sculpture of the Church of Akhthamar," The Art Bulletin, XXV (1943), 346-57. L. A. Durnovo, Brief History of Ancient Armenian Painting (in Russian) Erevan, 1957.

</td>
</tr>
<tr>
<td>

c) Armenia became the first kingdom to adopt Christianity as a state religion, pioneering a style of church architecture which anticipates Western Gothic.

</td>
<td>

P. C. Gulesserian, The Armenian Church, New York: AMS Press, Inc., 1970.

</td>
</tr>
<tr>
<td>

d) Christian Armenia was the heir to a long tradition of ancient lore and learning.

</td>
<td>

Leon Surmelian, Apples of Immortality: Folktales of Armenia, London: 1968. K. Sarkissian, A Brief Introduction to Armenian Christian Literature, London: 1960.

</td>
</tr>
</table>

(1) The chants and hymns played a prominent part in the cults of pagan Armenia; the priests and priestesses and other deities were accomplished singers.

(2) Music was also featured in the theatrical performances.

(Ancient sculptures and friezes show musicians performing on various instruments, while medieval manu-scripts often feature quaint little figures playing pipes and flutes.) Zabelle C. Boyajian, Armenian Legends and Poems, 2nd ed., London, 1958. (Also read the poems written by Moses of Khoren.)

(3) Poetry was very popular among the Armenian people. There were many prolific poets and theologians who wrote poetry.

(4) Armenians wrote short stories and novels which were famous among the civilized peoples of the world.

B. The history of the Armenian-American in the United States is a part of his more immediate cultural heritage, and is evidence of his own American identity.

1. The Armenians who first arrived in the U.S. intended to settle permanently.

Vartan Malcom, The Armenians in America, Boston: Pilgrim Press, 1919, pp. 1-15.

34

| *Study Outline* | *Notes and Sources* |
|---|---|
| a) Armenians came from different countries of the world. | (The U.S. Bureau of Immigration did not classify immigrants by nationality until after 1898, but by country of origin. Thus, Armenians were classified as Turks, Greeks, Persians, or whatever country they came from.) |
| b) Many reasons forced them to begin immigrating to America. | |
| (1) American missionaries in Turkey influenced many Armenians to emigrate to the United States. | Vartan Malcom, The Armenians in America, p. 66. (The early immigrants came individually not as a group or with their families.) |
| (2) They came to escape the religious persecutions, attrocities, and political pressures of various sorts. | Gary A. Kulhanjian, The Historical & Sociological Aspects of Armenian Immigration to the United States: 1890-1930, San Francisco, California: R & E Research Associates, 1975, pp. 3-6. |
| | Dickran H. Boyajian, Armenia: The Case for a Forgotten Genocide, New Jersey: Educational Book Crafters, 1972. |
| | George Horton, The Blight of Asia, New York: The Bobbs-Merril Company, Inc., 1953. |

| Study Outline | Notes and Sources |
|---|---|

(3) Many Armenian immigrants came to America in search of freedom, security and a better life for themselves and their families.

2. After 1600 A.D. Armenian immigrants began arriving in the United States.

a) Records indicate that Martin the Armenian was the first to settle in Virginia in 1609.

(Martin the Armenian was a tobacco expert.)

b) By 1863, there were only 40 Armenians in the United States.

James H. Tashjian, The Armenians of the United States and Canada, Boston, Massachusetts: Hairenik Press, 1947, Reprint 1970 by R & E Research Associates, p. 15.

c) Between 1834 and 1894, from 3,000 to 5,000 Armenians came to America.

(This figure is an approximation calculated from the total of 9,472 immigrants listed as originating from Turkey in the book The Armenians in America by Vartan Malcom, p. 65.)

d) In 1895, there was sudden influx of 2,767 Armenians to the U.S. and by 1898, a total of 15,913 immigrants had arrived in the U.S., largely as a result of the Hamidean Massacres.

Sarkis Atamian, The Armenian Community, New York: Philosophical Library, 1955, pp. 353-54.

e) From 1899 to 1917, 55,000 more

| *Study Outline* | *Notes and Sources* |
|---|---|

Armenians arrived in the U.S.
raising the total to 70,000.

f) Between 1920 and 1931, 26,146 Armenian immigrants came to America and many settled in large eastern cities of the United States.

James H. Tashjian, The Armenians of the United States and Canada, pp. 19-25.

g) By 1947, the total Armenian population was approximately 215,000 with an additional 8,000 in Canada.

h) In 1976, there were approximately 400,000 Armenian Americans in the United States.

Sarkis H. Kash, Crime Unlimited, Milwaukee, Wisconsin: Journal Printing Company, 1965, 82-95.

3. Armenian family patterns and traditions influenced the homelife of Armenian Americans, but later such patterns and traditions were strongly influenced by American culture.

a) At first, as a rule, Armenians married in their own ethnic group, but later, marriages with American girls of different extracts became common.

b) Marriages were arranged through relatives and parents. (Contem-

(The patriarchal family life of Armenians has played a major part in

37

| Study Outline | Notes and Sources |
|---|---|

porary marriage patterns are much
more like those of other Americans.)

the cultural identification of these
people in the United States.)

c) Activities and friendships were
   family and church-centered.

d) Scarcity of suitable Armenian
   girls in the U.S. compelled many
   young Armenians to bring girls
   from the old country.

(Consequently, an Armenian girl,
regardless of her beauty or station
in life, need have no fear of becoming a spinster.)

e) Many Armenian young men looked to
   other American girls to provide
   some of the needs which would
   ordinarily be met in a family.

f) Later generations found chances
   for normal family life improved.

(Inter-marriage with other Americans
improved the family life.)

g) From the beginning, there were
   fewer illiterates among the Armenian immigrants than any other
   immigrant groups.

h) Second and third generation
   Armenian-Americans devoted themselves to education and entering
   the professions.

James H. Tashjian, The Armenians
of the U.S. and Canada, 1947.

4. With professional training and education to match or surpass any
   other group Armenian-Americans have

38

attained high positions in industry, education, politics and business.

5. Due to their philosophical and religious outlook and their strong middle class values they assimilated easily in the American society.

(The middle class orientation was one of the characteristics distinguishing Armenians from other ethnic groups.)

6. At present, Armenian Americans are more interested in their ancient cultural heritage and beginning to study more about it; at the same time they are enriching their own American culture.

C. The perceptions and images of White Anglo-Saxon Protestants effected the Armenian Americans' perception of themselves.

1. There were positive perceptions.

a) Many employers felt that Armenians were good and honest workers.

(Industrial authorities and government labor spokesmen have declared that the Armenian workman was among the most industrious of workers.)

b) As Christians, they reflected the values of American society.

(The Armenian immigrant had learned that the surest way to advance in a chosen field was through pure, unadulterated, honest, unstinting hard work.)

| *Study Outline* | *Notes and Sources* |
|---|---|

(1) Armenian-American children re-
spected authority and behaved
well in the society.

(2) The patriarchal family life of       Gary A. Kulhanjian, <u>An Abstract of</u>
Armenians played a major part          <u>the Historical and Sociological</u>
in taking care of the family.          <u>Aspects of Armenian Immigration to</u>
Mothers gave help and stability        <u>the U.S., 1890-1930</u>, pp. 29-30.
to the home life of family
members.

(3) Most of the parents sacrificed
their own welfare to educate the
children; and their children, in
return, felt a reciprocal obligation.

(4) Most Armenians had a strong
sense of obligation to the
family as well as to the community.

(5) The history of the Armenians in      (Many Americans of Armenian ancestry
America is full of Horatio Alger       were stereotyped as having wealthy
stories.  These aspirations for        rug businesses.)
high achievement and status were
consistent with American ideals.

2.  There were some negative stereotypes
of Armenian-Americans.

a) Some labor organizations viewed them as a threat.

   (1) They worked long hours for low pay.

   (2) They were very competitive because employers liked their attitudes and efficiency.

D. From the very beginning of their arrival in the United States, Armenian-Americans contributed tremendously to the cultural and material progress of America.

1. Armenian laborers worked in building of the railroads and helped develop the tobacco, silk, and raisin industries in the United States.

(They were instrumental in establishing the rug industry in the United States.)

2. Armenian-Americans have made notable contributions to American war efforts.

(Civil War, Spanish-American War of 1898, World War I and World War II.)

   a) Armenian-Americans served in Spanish American War of 1898.

James H. Tashjian, The Armenians of the U.S. and Canada, pp. 54-59.

   b) Armenian-American youth distinguished itself by heroic actions in all places where the United States sent its military and

(Lt. Earnest Devrishian of Richmond, Virginia, holds the Congressional Medal of Honor for heroic action while a sergeant in Italy.

41

naval forces.

c)  The list of heroes is too long to include here.

d)  Many Armenian-Americans performed well in the Korean and Vietnam wars.

Stanley Maligian died in the skies over Belgium during an airborne operation.

The first American soldier to die in the invasion of North Africa was an Armenian, Lt. Koushnarian.

Other names worth mentioning are: Lt. Victor Maghakian, the Derian twins, Albert and Robert.  They fought in World War II.)

E.  Many Armenian Americans have made out-standing contributions to America and to the world in all fields of knowl-edge.

- Anahid Ajemian, Concert Violinist

- Maro Ajemian, Concert Pianist

- Levon Akopiontz, noted surgeon

- A. Amerikian, Engineer

- Paolo Ananian, Basso, Metropolitan Opera

- Mardiros Ananikian, Professor and writer

- K. Arakelian, Industrialist

- Artine Artinian, Professor and Writer

- Vahan S. Babasinian, scientist

- A. I. Bezzerides, Writer

- A. H. Bubbulian, Inventor of high altitude oxygen mask

- Carl Calousd, Painter

- Vahan Cardashian, Distinguished attorney

- H. H. Chakmakjian, Biochemist

- Thomas Corwin, American Statesman

- Harry Daghlian, Researcher in atomic energy

- Noobar Danielian, U.S. Department of Commerce

- Leon Danieloff, Ballet Dancer

- Reuben Darbinian, Journalist and Author

- Christopher der Seropian, Discoverer of the green and black of American

  dollar bill

- Sirarpe Der Nersessian, Professor of Byzantine art and lecturer

- Leon Dominian, Geographer and diplomat

- Arshag Fetvajian, Distinguished artist and archaeologist

- Arlene Francis, Radio actress

- Mugurdich Garo, Photographer

- Menas Gregory, Psychologist

- Raymon Hitchcock, Actress, stage name Flora Zabelle

- Alan Hovaness, Composer

- Arshag Karageuzian, Carpet manufacturer

- Vahan Kalenderian, New York Attorney

- Vladimir Karapetoff, Professor of Electrical Engineering

- Mihran Kasabian, Pioneer roentgenologist

- Sarkis Katchadourian, Painter

- M. Katcharoff, Ballet Dancer

- Varaztad Kazanjian, Distinguished Plastic Surgeon

- Arthur Kevorkian, Mycologist

- H. M. D. Malejian, Surgeon

- Pascal Marjian, Dean of American Catholic Church in America

- Rouben Mamoulian, Distinguished stage and screen director

- M. Mangassarian, Preacher and orator

- George Markikian, Culinary artist and author

- Archbishop Tirayr Nersoyan, Head of Apostolic Church in America

- David Paige, Artist of an Admiral Byrd expedition to the Antarctica

- Haig Patigian, Distinguished sculptor

- Hovsep Pushman, Painter

- A. O. Sarkisian, Scholar and author

- William Saroyan, Outstanding writer and playwright

- General Sebouh, Patriot and soldier

- Manasseh G. Sevag, Chemist

- General Haig Shakerjian, Brig. Gen., U.S. Army

- Leon Surmelian, Writer

- Armand Tokatyan, Distinguished Tenor, Metropolitan Opera

- Manuel Tolegian, Painter

- Aram Torossian, Scholar and writer

- Tamara Toumanova, Ballet Dancer

- Moosegh Vigonny, Developed synthetic method of converting grape sugar into
  tartaric acid

- Luise Vosgerchian, Concert Pianist

- Simon Vratzian, Distinguished patriot ; former Prime Minister of the Armenian
  Independent Republic

- Hratch Yervant, Editor, "Baikar Daily"

- the Brothers Ziljian, Famous Cymbal manufacturers

44

F.  Recently some Armenian Americans are
    trying to bring an increasing aware-
    ness of Armenian question in the
    United States and the atrocities com-
    mitted against them by the Turkish
    government.

PART II:  ARMENIAN AMERICAN CONFLICT

I.  Introduction

Armenian-Americans, as other immigrant groups who came to America from middle east and Asia, were victims of prejudice when they first arrived, so they banded together for security and identity.

Many Americans were intolerant of differences in food habits, entertainment, church affiliation, etc.  These attitudes and prejudices of other Americans created conflict among Armenian immigrants.

The second generation Armenian-American had the usual cultural and linguistic conflicts to deal with.  He was discriminated against in employment and other areas.  Slowly, through hard work and education, they overcame some of the prejudices and discriminations.

II.  Guide and Sourcebook

| *Study Outline* | *Notes and Sources* |
|---|---|
| A.  It was a type of conflict--the struggle to make a living and to escape the attrocities--which brought the great mass of Armenian immigrants to America, where they thought to find means to better conditions for themselves and their families. | James H. Tashjian, The Armenians of the United States and Canada, Massachusetts:  Hairenik Press, 1947, pp. 1-20. |
| 1.  To escape religious persecutions and atrocities at home they made the decision to emigrate to America. | (Tashjian presents three phases of Armenian immigration to North America.) |
| 2.  Another reason was to better themselves and their families economically and socially. | |
| B.  Armenian settlers who immigrated to the United States were subjected to | |

46

discrimination and injustice.

1. Discrimination had been prevalent against Armenian immigrants in jobs and other areas.

    (There were isolated cases of discrimination against Armenian immigrants.)

2. The 1924 Immigration Act discriminated against Armenian Americans. Later, it was decided that Armenians were not of Asiatic descent and thus eligible for naturalization as American citizens.

    United States v. Cartozian, Federal Report (2d) 919, July 27, 1925.

    (The United States Government sued for the annulment of the naturalization papers of Tatos O. Cartozian, a rug manufacturer in Portland, Oregon. The government believed that Armenians were "ineligible to citizenship" because of their Asiatic descent. Later they were considered as members of the "Alpine" race and were eligible to naturalization as American citizens.)

    See also: "Decides for Armenians," New York Times, July 28, 1925, p. 12:8.

3. The 1924 Immigration Act curbed aliens of each nationality and gave preference to those people who came from northern and western Europe.

    (Armenians had no quota of their own but came to the United States on the quotas of their home countries which were comparatively small in relation to the quotas of other groups in the United States without much difficulty.)

C. In 1965, Lyndon B. Johnson signed an

    (Highly educated Armenian professionals

| Study Outline | Notes and Sources |
|---|---|
| immigration bill to eliminate the quota system which was weighted in favor of north Europeans.  This paved the way for many Armenians to immigrate to the United States. | and entrepreneurs were able to immigrate to the United States without much difficulty.) |

PART III: INTEGRATION VERSUS NATIONALISM
ARMENIAN AMERICAN DILEMMA

I.  Introduction

Most Armenian immigrants had strong nationalistic feelings. They maintained their ties with their families and kinfolk in the old country of their ancestors. Some of the early immigrants anticipated returning to their countries after earning enough money.

Discriminatory immigration laws strengthened the cultural ties among the Armenians around the world.

Later generations of Armenian-Americans have not strongly identified themselves with past traditions and customs. Many have detached themselves from the cultural practices of their parents and grandparents. The assimilation process influenced Armenian-American young people in America.

The present status of Armenian Americans is much like other cultural minority groups in America. Most young Armenian-Americans have internalized the middle-class values of America and form a part of American pluralistic society.

II.  Source and Guidebook

| *Study Outline* | *Notes and Sources* |
|---|---|
| A.  The Armenian immigrants like many other immigrant groups clung to and perpetuated their cultural identity. | Francis J. Brown and Joseph S. Roucek, One America, New York: Prentice-Hall, Inc., 1945, p. 302. (The real strength of Armenian cultural identity has been the Armenian church in America as well as in the world.) |
| 1.  Cultural ties and religious beliefs prompted Armenian Americans to group together not only in America but also in the world. | |
| 2.  Many difficulties--new country, different people, a difficult | |

language and loneliness--forced
Armenian immigrants to band together.

3. Many of the Armenian Americans supported their families, religious
   and educational institutions in
   the old country.

B. Discrimination and discriminatory
   laws intensified nationalistic feelings of Armenian-Americans.

(Discrimination had been evident in
the immigration policy of 1921 and
discrimination against Americans of
Armenian ancestry existed in several
areas.)

1. Armenian businessmen preferred
   their kinsmen as workers.

2. Armenian churches and political
   organizations maintained the
   nationalistic leadership of
   Armenian-Americans.

3. Many Armenian-American publications
   helped to maintain Armenian solidarity and friendship.

4. Armenian-American nationalism which
   identified with the Armenian homeland was thwarted by the events of
   1916 in Turkey.

5. Many Armenian Americans strongly

feel that a homeland inside Turkey

should be established.

C. American born Armenians detached            Gary A. Kulhanjian, The Historical

themselves most of all from the cul-           and Sociological Aspects of Ar-

tural patterns of their parents and            menian Immigration to the U.S.:

grandparents. They began to ask for            1890-1930, p. 24.

integration and a full participation

in the American main stream.

1. The younger Armenian-American who

is born in America, accepted the

American way of life. This created

a cultural gap between his immi-

grant parents and himself.

2. The immigrants had taught their

children to ask for equal rights

and opportunities in America.

a) The work ethic of the immigrants

conformed to the middle class

values of America.

b) Traditional family life of Arme-

nians discouraged juvenile delin-

quency and encouraged respect for

authority and law.

c) Young Armenian-Americans utilized

the educational facilities and

surpassed all other groups in

terms of number of years of

school completed.

D.  In recent years there has developed

a new Armenian-American nationalism

to express concern about injustice

and repression against Armenians in

their homelands.


## Conclusion

The Armenian Americans who settled in the United States immigrated to America to be free from religious and political persecutions and to better conditions for themselves and their families.  The span of Armenian American history is shorter than that of other minority groups in America.

The Armenian immigrants brought with them rich ancient cultures and have contributed immensely in philosophy, religion, literature, music, art, technologies and other areas of human achievement.

Armenian Americans had their own cultural identities and were able to maintain those identities by organizing various political, scholastic, philanthropic and religious groups.  Gradually, however, they integrated completely into the American society.

# BIBLIOGRAPHY

Armenag, Sakisian. "Notes on the Sculpture of the Church of Akhthamar." The Art Bulletin, XXV (1943).

Atamian, Sarkis. The Armenian Community. New York: Philosophical Library, 1955.

Boyajian, Dickran H. Armenia: The Case for a Forgotten Genocide. New Jersey: Educational Book Crafters, 1972.

Boyajian, Zabelle C. Armenian Legends and Poems. 2nd ed. London: 1958.

Brown, Francis J. and Roucek, Joseph S. One America. New York: Prentice-Hall, Inc., 1945.

Durnovo, L. A. A Brief History of Ancient Armenian Painting (in Russian), Erevan, 1957.

Gulesserian, P. C. The Armenian Church. New York: AMS Press, Inc., 1970.

Hamilton, J. Arnott. Byzantine Architecture and Decoration. London: 1935.

Horton, George. The Blight of Asia. New York: The Bobbs-Merril Co., Inc., 1953.

Kash, Sarkis H. Crime Unlimited. Milwaukee, Wisconsin: Journal Printing Co., 1965.

Kulhanjian, Gary. The Historical & Sociological Aspects of Armenian Immigration to the United States: 1890-1930. San Francisco, California: R & E Research Associates, Inc., 1975.

Long, David M. Armenia: Cradle of Civilization. London: George Allen and Unwin, Ltd., 1970.

Malcom, Vartan. The Armenians in America. Boston: Pilgrim Press, 1919.

New York Times, "Decides for Armenians," July 28, 1925.

Sarkissian, K. A Brief Introduction to Armenian Christian Literature. London: 1960.

Strzygowski, Joseph. Origin of Christian Church Art. Oxford, England: 1923.

Surmelian, Leon. Apples of Immortality: Folktales of Armenia. London: 1968.

Tashjian, James H. The Armenians of the United States and Canada. Boston, Massachusetts: Hairenik Press, 1947.

53

PART I:  MIDDLE EASTERN AMERICAN IDENTITY

I.  Introduction

The emphasis is on Middle Eastern immigrants (Syrian-Lebanese) who came to
the United States from the Middle East.  According to some estimates there are more
than 850,000 Middle-Eastern Christian Americans in the United States.

The Middle Easterners brought with them a rich and proud history.  They made
brilliant contributions to the world culture in all fields of human endeavor.

Immigrants from Middle Eastern countries may be characterized as absorbing
American values and social structures.

There was much in Middle Eastern philosophy and tradition that have made assimilation an easy process.  Standards of hard work, discipline, and ethics were very
similar to those of Anglo-Saxon Protestant America.

As an ethnic group, Middle Eastern Americans have distinguished themselves
in many ways, and have earned a place of respect in America's pluralistic society.

II.  Guide and Sourcebook

| *Study Outline* | *Notes and Sources* |
|---|---|
| A. Middle Eastern Americans who migrated to the United States were products of distinguished ancient cultures. | Philip K. Hitti, History of the Arabs, 10th edition, London:  Macmillan, 1070. |
| 1. Middle Eastern Civilization is very ancient and has contributed im- mensely to the world culture. | (By 2700 B.C. there had emerged a Middle Eastern Civilization with a strong centralized government, a com- plex form of writing as well as the paper and ink with which to write, the beginnings of scientific medical diagnosis, and the first calendar of 365 days.) |
| a) They were responsible for many discoveries and inventions which | |

54

enhanced the advancement of technology in the world.

b) Middle Eastern art, painting, sculpture and architecture has been
recognized as among the best in
history.

c)  In religion and philosophy,
Middle Easterners have influenced much of the world.

(Eastern Christianity is composed
principally of Eastern Orthodox
Christians and Roman Catholics of
the Eastern rites, i.e., Melkites,
Maronites and others.  There are cer-
tain heretical groups, such as the
Monophysites, the Nestorians and the
Jacobites.)

(1) Middle Eastern Christianity per-
ceive and conceptualize reality
differently than western Christianity.  They are oriented
toward the mysterious and the
spiritual.

(2) They are usually "other-world"
directed and not overly concerned with "this-world" ob-
jectives.

"Christianity in the Arab East," The
Link, November/December, 1973.

(3) Christian ideals were loyalty,
chastity, selflessness and

55

service to others; a Christian's
primary duty was to uphold the
ideals of Christianity.

d) Middle Easterners had well developed musical, artistic, and
literary traditions.

(1) Middle Eastern visual art is
decorative.

(2) The highest achievement of the
Middle Easterners was in poetry
and rhetoric.

e) Middle Eastern culture also provided a strong sense of identity
to Middle Easterners and their
American-born children.

B. The history of the Middle Eastern in
America is a part of his more immediate cultural heritage, and is evidence of his own American identity.

1. Several factors influenced Middle
Easterners to migrate to American
shores.

a) Immediately before the era of mass
immigration to America, a Catholic
Melkite-rite bishop came to
America in 1849 to solicit funds

Yves Congar, After Nine Hundred
Years, New York:  Fordham University
Press, 1957.

"Arab-Adventures in the New World,"
Yearbook, 1965-66, New York:  The
Action Committee on American Arab
Relations, 1966.

Philip M. Kayal and Joseph M. Kayal,
The Syrian-Lebanese in America, Massa-
chusettes:  Twayne Publishers, 1975,
p. 61.

| *Study Outline* | *Notes and Sources* |
|---|---|

to reconstruct Saint John's Monastery in Khonshara, Syria Lebanon).

b) They came to America to escape economic stagnation and low standards of living for themselves and their families.

c) The news of economic opportunities brought many Middle Easterners to America.

Norman Duncan, "A People from the East," Harper's Magazine, March 1903, p. 554.

d) A substantial emigration to America occurred between 1890 and 1914 as a result of renewed Turkish oppression.

(Between 1900 and 1914, 100,000 Lebanese emigrated to the four corners of the world.)

E. J. Dillon, "Turkey's Plight," The Contemporary Review, July 1913, pp. 123, 128.

e) From 1869 to 1898, 20,690 Middle Eastern immigrants came from greater Syria.

International Migration Statistics, Vol. I, National Bureau of Economic Research, Inc., 1925.

Between 1899 and 1932, 106,391 immigrants came from Syria to the United States.

Annual Reports of Commissioner General of Immigration, 1926-1933.

f) The Quota Law which has been implemented since 1924 was a factor in limiting Middle Eastern immigrant to the United States.

| *Study Outline* | *Notes and Sources* |
|---|---|

g)  After World War II, the immigration restrictions were relaxed.
This facilitated the immigration
of Middle Easterners to America.

Morrow Berger, "America's Syrian
Community," Commentary, 25 (4) (April
1958), p. 314.

h)  A great proportion of the students
from the Middle East who came to
study in the United States stayed
to work in America after completing their studies.

i)  In 1970 there were more than
850,000 Middle Eastern Americans
in the United States.

(This is an estimate based on the
population of 1.66 million Arab-
Americans in the United States.)

2.  The Middle Eastern-family patterns
and traditions influenced (and are
still influencing) the home life of
Middle Eastern Americans, but such
patterns and traditions were
strongly affected by American culture.

a)  In the beginning, marriages were
not usually the western style.

R. P. Davies, "Syrian Arabic Kinship
Terms," Southwestern Journal of
Anthropology, Vol. 3, No. 3 (Autumn
1949), pp. 244-252.

b)  The Middle Eastern Christians do
not resist inter-ethnic marriage
with Americans, generally, they

encourage this trend.

c) Activities, friendships, and employment were family centered.

(The Middle Eastern families tended
to be tight, self-contained, self-
sufficient units controlled by parental authority. Family organization followed patterns which in many
ways remained unchanged generation
after generation.)

d) Second and third generation
Middle Eastern Americans concerned themselves with education
and with entering the professions. More stress had been
placed on the professions and
education.

Barbara C. Aswad, ed., Arabic
Speaking Communities in American
Cities, New York: The Center for
Migration Studies of New York, Inc.,
1974, pp. 35-36.

3. The educated, highly professional
Middle Eastern Americans occupy
prominent positions in American
society.

Joseph R. Haiek, The American Arabic
Speaking Community:  1975 Almanac,
Los Angeles, California:  The News
Circle, 1975.

P. M. Kayal and J. M. Kayal, The
Syrian-Lebanese in America:  A Study
in Religion and Assimilation, Op. Cit.,
pp. 89-111.

C. America created its own definition of
Middle Eastern American identity,
which varied from time to time, from

group to group, and which had varying

psychological effects on Middle East-

ern American's perception of them-

selves.

1. There were positive stereotypes.

   a) Employers viewed them as good and honest workers.

Adele Younis, "The Arabs who Followed Columbus," Yearbook, 1965-1966, New York: The Action Committee on American Arab Relations, 1966.

      (1) They worked long hours under difficult conditions.

Elaine Hagopian and Ann Paden (eds.), The Arab-Americans: Studies in Assimilation, Wilmette, Illinois: The Medina University Press Inter-National, 1969, pp. 106-107.

      (2) They were successful in their economic pursuits.

   b) The Middle Easter-American religious and family traditions fit in well with American cultural patterns.

(The Middle Easterners who immigrated to America were Christians by faith and composed principally of Eastern Orthodox Christians and Roman Catholics of the Eastern rites.)

      (1) Middle Eastern-American children behaved well and treated parents and authorities with respect.

(They seemed to be typically American: they were frugal, religious, non-criminal, industrious, mobile and dedicated.)

      (2) Middle Eastern families were

Affif I. Tannous, The Arab Village

60

| *Study Outline* | *Notes and Sources* |
|---|---|
| close knit and the members displayed solidarity that seemed admirable. | Community in the Middle East, Washington, D.C.: Smithsonian Institute, 1943, p. 537. |
| (3) The patriarchal family placed the father in the position of authority and the mother gave stability to the home by answering to the physical and emotional needs of the children. | Philip Hitti, Syrians in America, New York: George Doran, 1924. |
| (4) Most of them felt a strong sense of duty to their community and family. | Cecyle S. Neidle, The New Americans, New York: Twayne Publishers, 1967. |
| (5) Desires for status and high standards of achievement were consistent with American ideals, though such standards often led to conflicts. | Louise Houghton, "Syrians in the United States," The Survey, Part I, July 1, 1911, p. 493, Part II, pp. 653, 654, 663, 664. |

2. There were negative views of Middle Eastern Americans' competitiveness.

  a) Willingness to work long hours in his own business posed a threat to many native businessmen.

| | |
|---|---|
| (1) Middle Eastern women (Syrian) who were often employed in family-controlled businesses, | Reports of the Industrial Commission, Vol. XV, pp. 443, 445. |

were counter to the ideals of
American women.

(2) The efficiency of Middle Eastern
workers through peddling tar-
nished their image in the eyes
of native Americans.

(3) Native American businessmen felt
that the Middle Easterners were
potentially dangerous rivals because they use their employment
to learn the business and set up
competing concerns.

b) Negative stereotypes developed.

(1) Some of the stereotypes associated with Middle Easterners
were: wild-eyed Syrians, fakirs,
and peddlers.

(2) Newspapers and law enforcing
agencies exploited the negative
stereotypes and fears.

New York Times, May 27, 1902, and
October 24, 1905.
New York Herald, October 29, 1905.
(In 1902 and 1905 two violent situa-
tions in New York City reached the
attention of police and the general
public.)

(3) Negative Stereotypes slowly
gave way to accurate descriptions

Adele Younis, "The Coming of the
Arabic-Speaking People to the United

of their life-styles and cul-          States," Op. Cit., pp. 303-304.

ture.

D.  Many Middle Eastern Americans have

    made outstanding contributions to

    their country and to the world in all

    fields of human endeavor.

1.  Middle Eastern Americans in Science

    - Dr. Nicholas S. Assali, Professor of Obstetrics

    - Dr. Michael E. DeBakey, Heart Surgeon, a pioneer in Cardiovascular disease

      surgery.  He was the first to use a heart pump successfully on a patient.

    - Dr. Robert G. Monsour, specialist in psychiatry and neurology

    - Dr. Alexander A. Kirkish, well known dentist

    - Dr. Howard P. Monsour, Suregon

    - Dr. Roy C. Monsour, medical doctor

    - Dr. William J. Monsour, specialist in cardiology

    - Dr. George Doumani, geologist

2.  In politics Middle Eastern Americans are beginning to provide leadership

    - James Abourezk, U.S. Senator from South Dakota

    - Abraham Kazen, U.S. Congressman from Texas

    - Jim Abdnor, U.S. Congressman from Nebraska

    - Toby Moffett, U.S. Congressman from Connecticut

    - Ralph Nader, Consumer crusader

    - James R. Deeb, State Senator in Florida

    - Thomas L. Hazouri, State Congressman in Florida

    - Edward Hanna, Mayor of Utica, New York

    - James J. Tayoun, State Congressman in Pennsylvania

- Victor Atiyeh, Oregon State Senator

- George Kasem, Oregon State House of Representatives

- Elias Francis, Lieutenant Governor of New Mexico

3. Scholars

- Clement J. Nouri, Educator, Dean, School of Business Administration, University of San Diego, California

- Many others

4. Entertainment, Broadcasting

- William J. Baroody, President, American Enterprise Institute

- George Oliver Cory, Broadcast Executive

- Edmonde Alex Haddad, Radio Commentator

- Mardi Rustam, Movie Producer, actor, president of International Film Lab. Inc.

- Danny Thomas, actor and entertainer

- Many others

5. Enterpreneurs, Businessmen

- Earnest George, Businessman

- Minor George, Enterpreneur

- Dan Hanna, Portland enterpreneur

- George Maloof, Real estate broker

- Frank Maria, Management consultant

- John Shaheen, enterpreneur

- Thelma Shain, enterpreneur

- Nicholas Shammas, enterpreneur

- Anthony Abraham, owner of one of the world's largest retail automobile dealerships

- Robert S. Andrews, enterpreneur

- B. D. Eddie, businessman

- Raymond Jallow, chief economist and enterpreneur

- Norman N. Mamey, enterpreneur

- Frank E. Swyden, businessman

- Woodrow W. Woody, enterpreneur

- Harry Zachary, enterpreneur

6. Writers

- William Peter Blatty, author of best selling books

- Helen E. Corey, author of a best seller

- Samuel Hazo, professor, poet and writer

- Labeebee J. H. Saquet, writer

PART II:  SYRIAN AND LEBANESE AMERICAN CONFLICT

I.  Introduction

The Middle Eastern immigrants and their children had the usual cultural and linguistic conflicts to deal with in America.  And, like many other newcomers, they encountered hardships and earned their way through persistence and hard work as laborers, businessmen, store keepers and peddlers.  Later, many were successful in establishing themselves as politicians, businessmen, entrepreneurs and professionals.

In the absence of any physical or racial distinction to reveal their Middle Eastern origin, the second and third generations found themselves fully accepted by the American society.


II.  Guide and Sourcebook

| *Study Outline* | *Notes and Sources* |
| --- | --- |
| A.  It was a type of conflict--the struggle to make a living and also to escape the military oppression and religious persecution--which brought the Middle Eastern immigrants to America where he thought to find means to better conditions for his family. | (A large number of Christians have migrated to the United States in the past half century.) |
| 1.  Many Middle Eastern people came to America to escape religious persecution and political oppression. | |
| 2.  Many intended to make the greatest possible amount of money and return to their homeland. | |
| B.  The immigrants who came to America encountered hardships but earned their way through persistence and hard work | Habib Katibah, "Syrian Americans," in Brown and Rocek, One America, Op. Cit., pp. 286-287. |

66

as peddlers, storekeepers and laborers.

1. After coming to America, the economically oriented Middle Easterners
   became merchants, white collar
   workers and professionals.

Edward Corsi, The Shadow of Liberty,
New York:  Macmillan Co., 1935, pp.
261-266.

2. Some of them opened factories, im-
   porting houses, travel bureaus,
   steamship companies, real estate
   brokerages, import-export businesses,
   restaurants, and bars.

P. M. Kayal and J. M. Kayal, The
Syrian-Lebanese in America, Op. Cit.,
pp. 96-111.

C. Practices within the Middle Eastern
   American communities led to personal
   or group conflict.

1. Sometimes tensions between Catholic
   and Orthodox Christian groups were
   very high.  Tensions existed within
   groups also.

(In 1902 and 1905, there was violence
in New York City between Catholic
Maronites and the Orthodox over con-
trol of the community's press.)

2. Later immigrations were curtailed by
   the coming of World War I.

Robert A. Divine, American Immigration
Policy 1924-1952, New York:  Plenum,
1971.

3. The immigration law of 1924, assigned a small quota to Middle
   Eastern countries.

4. The passage of the Immigration and
   Naturalization Act of 1965, relaxed
   the immigration restrictions of
   Middle Easterners by abolishing the
   quota system.

(This bill was signed by President
Lyndon B. Johnson in 1965.)

PART III:  INTEGRATION VS. NATIONALISM
MIDDLE EASTERN AMERICAN DILEMMA

I.   Introduction

Most Middle Eastern immigrants had strong nationalistic sentiments in the beginning.  Some of them maintained cultural and family ties in the Middle East and also supported families and relatives in the old country.

First generation Middle Eastern immigrants shared a common culture and language.  However, these immigrants did not reflect all the social groupings in the Middle East.  They formed ethnic enclaves for the sake of survival in American society.

Later generations did not acquire strong cultural ties with the countries of their parents.  Instead, they took the course of cultural and racial assimilation. It is of interest to note that later generations chose America as their home and had no sense of Middle Eastern nationalism.

II.  Guide and Sourcebook

| *Study Outline* | *Notes and Sources* |
|---|---|
| A.  Early Middle Eastern Americans held tenaciously to their cultural identity and to the hope of return to the Middle East for living with their families and relatives. | Morris Zelditch, "The Syrians in Pittsburgh," Unpublished M.A. Dissertation, University of Pittsburgh, Pennsylvania, 1936, p. 39. |
| 1.  The early Middle Eastern immigrants clustered in smaller cities and towns for the sake of survival in the American society. | (They essentially followed the patterns of other ethnic groups by settling and concentrating in urban areas.  Today a vast majority of all Middle Eastern Christian Americans live in the industrialized Northeast.) |
| 2.  Faced with the language barrier, early Middle Eastern immigrants found it natural to form their own small communities. | |

| *Study Outline* | *Notes and Sources* |
|---|---|

3. Loyalty of Middle Eastern Americans to their families and relatives was reflected in their financial support of families and community institutions.

4. Many Middle Eastern Americans still maintain close ties with the homeland by observing the religious and cultural traditions of the old country.

B. The United States' national policies and the Israeli-Arab controversy in the Middle East do generate nationalistic feelings among Middle Eastern Americans.

1. Generally they are reluctant to get involved in international Arab affairs.

2. Many Middle Eastern Americans are

Elaine C. Hagopian, "The Institutional Development of the Arab-American Community in Boston," in The Arab Americans by E. C. Hagopian and Ann Paden, eds., p. 69.

(The Middle Eastern American community belongs to various religious denominations. Most of the pioneering Christian immigrants followed a number of Eastern rite denominations, mainly, Antiochian, Orthodox, Maronites, Melkites, Copts, Syrians, Assyrians, and Chaldeans. Each denomination is grouped around its church and these can be found in all major urban centers of the United States.)

(The Middle Eastern Americans have not generally been active politically, and hence could effectively influence neither the news coverage of the conflict nor the orientation of the American political establishment.)

Morroe Berger, "America's Syrian Community," Commentary, 24:4, April 1958, p. 319.

(Large Christian groups in the United

| *Study Outline* | *Notes and Sources* |
|---|---|
| still suspicious of the intentions of the Moslems. | States still remember their inferior status under the Moslem Turks and their uneasy relations with the Moslems in general. |
| 3. The Middle Eastern Christian Americans still feel that the Middle East discriminated against them socially. | P. M. Kayal and J. M. Kayal, The Syrian-Lebanese in America, Op. Cit., p. 223. |
| 4. It is ironical that many Middle Eastern Christian elites possess bitter feelings towards their countries of origin. | (Study the current conflicts in Lebanon between Christians and Moslems.) |
| 5. It seems that the Middle Eastern Americans will eventually abandon completely the cultural style and social life that characterize their ethnic history. | |

# MIDDLE EASTERN-AMERICAN BIBLIOGRAPHY

Annual Reports of Commissioner General of Immigration, 1926-1933.

"Arab-Adventures in the New World," Yearbook, 1965-66. New York: The Action Committee on American Arab Relations, 1966.

Aswad, Barbara C. Arabic-Speaking Communities in American Cities. New York: The Center for Migration Studies of New York, Inc., 1974.

Berger, Morrow. "America's Syrian Community." Commentary, 25:4, April 1958.

"Christianity in the Arab East." The Link, November/December 1973.

Congar, Yves. After Nine Hundred Years. New York: Fordham University Press, 1957.

Corsi, Edward. The Shadow of Liberty. New York: Macmillan Co., 1935.

Davies, R. P. "Syrian Arabic Kinship Terms." Southwestern Journal of Anthropology, Vol. 3, No. 3, Autumn 1949.

Dillon, E. J. "Turkey's Plight." The Contemporary Review, July 1913.

Divine, Robert A. American Immigration Policy: 1924-1952. New York: Plenum, 1971.

Duncan, Norman. "A People from the East." Harper's Magazine, March 1903.

Hagopian, Elaine and Paden, Ann., ed. The Arab-Americans: Studies in Assimilation. Wilmette, Illinois: The Medina University Press International, 1969.

Haiek, Joseph R. The American Arabic Speaking Community: 1975 Almanac. California: The News Circle, 1975.

Hitti, Philip K. History of the Arabs. London: Macmillan, 1970.

--"--"--          . Syrians in America. New York: George Doran, 1924.

Houghton, Louise. "Syrians in the United States." The Survey, Part I and Part II.

International Migration Statistics, Vol. I. National Bureau of Economic Research, Inc., 1925.

Katibah, Habib. "Syrian Americans." In Brown and Rocek, One America.

Neidle, Cecyle S. The New Americans. New York: Twayne Publishers, 1967.

New York Times, May 27, 1902, and October 24, 1905.

New York Herald. October 29, 1905.

Tannous, Affif I. The Arab Village Community in the Middle East. Washington, D.C.: Smithsonian Institute, 1943.

Younis, Adele.  "The Arabs Who Followed Columbus."  Yearbook, 1965-66.  New York: The Action Committee on American Arab Relations, 1966.

Zelditch, Morris.  "The Syrians in Pittsburgh."  Unpublished M.A. Dissertation. University of Pittsburgh, Pennsylvania, 1936.

Kayal, Philip M., and Kayal, Joseph M.  The Syrian-Lebanese in America.  Massachusetts:  Twayne Publishers, 1975.

PART I:  EAST INDIAN, PAKISTANI AND BANGLA
DESHI AMERICANS' IDENTITY

## I.  Introduction

This part of the volume is mainly concerned with those Americans whose ancestors originally came from the Indian subcontinent in search of good life for
themselves and their families, viz. Indians, Pakistanis and Bangla Deshis.

On August 15, 1947, British India was divided into two independent countries,
India and Pakistan.  Later, on December 16, 1971, the eastern part of Pakistan,
declared itself the free and independent nation of Bangla Desh.  Now there are
three independent countries on the subcontinent of India--India, Pakistan and
Bangla Desh.  At present, the total population of the subcontinent of India is
approximately 780 millions.

Here, the term "East Indian Americans" include Indians, Pakistanis and Bangla
Deshis.

The East Indian Americans who immigrated to America brought with them rich
ancient cultures.  Of course, cultures on the Indian subcontinent varied, but
there is much to be admired in their rich contributions to world culture in
philosophy and religions, in literature and the arts, in science and technology,
and in traditions, customs and social institutions.

The immigrants have sought to retain their East Indian identities, their
family ties and loyalties to the old country.  For a long time, discriminatory
laws in America made it difficult to keep up close ties with the old country and
also made identification with America impossible.

The East Indian immigrants have established themselves in this continent in
a relatively short time in the teeth of fierce competition.  Unlike other immigrants of a past era, East Indian immigrants usually have an excellent educational
background and possess special technical skills.  They have the largest number of
professionals in proportion to their total numbers--about 150,000 professionals.
Some of them have already been accorded recognition in America and the world.
These East Indian Americans are contributing to the enrichment of the economic,
spiritual and social life of the main stream of American society.  In the future,
they will make more contributions to American culture.

## II.  Guide and Sourcebook

| *Study Outline* | *Notes and Sources* |
|---|---|
| A.  The East Indian immigrants who came to America to settle belonged to one of the most interesting and important Civilizations of the world. | H. V. Srinivasa Murthy and S. U. Kamath, Studies in Indian Culture, New York: Asia Publishing House, 1973, 3-4. |

| Study Outline | Notes and Sources |
|---|---|
| 1. East Indian Civilization has a long and continuous history extending over 5000 years. | Percival Spear, India: A Modern History, Ann Arbor, Michigan: The University of Michigan Press, 1961, 27-38. |
| 2. The East Indian culture has contributed immensely to world culture. | |
| a) From the classical days of Greece and Rome, Indian cottons have been known and prized in Europe. | (To this day technical cotton terms betray their Eastern origin. Thus Calicoes are named after the port of Calicut in South India.) |
| b) The spice trade flourished long before the Christian era. | |
| c) In more recent times India has supplied indigo. | |
| d) Several drugs have been supplied by India, viz. cinnamon and opium. | |
| e) In the intellectual world India passed on her discoveries to the West via the Arab world. | (India has influenced the outside world in the subtler and deeper realms of imagination and thought.) |
| (1) The Hindu-Arabic numerals were developed in India. | |
| (2) By the 7th century, Hindus had devised a sign for zero and worked out a decimal system. In algebra they were also ahead. | Bency K. Sarkar, Hindu Achievement in Exact Science, New York: Longmans, Green & Co., 1918. Swami Akhilananda, Mental Health and Hindu Psychology, New York: Harper & |

| _Study Outline_ | _Notes and Sources_ |
|---|---|
| | Bros., 1951. |
| (3) India provided the material and the stimulus for the development of the new sciences of philology and comparative religion. | |
| f) East Indian art, painting, sculpture and architecture had gained a permanent place in the world. | S. Kramrisch, Indian Sculpture, London: 1937. |
| g) In religion and philosophy, East Indian thought has influenced much of the world. | Prabhu D. Shastra, The Essentials of Eastern Philosophy, New York: The Macmillan Co., 1928. (Hinduism is a body of customs and a body of ideas, the two having such pervasive power and defensive force as to absorb or resist passively for centuries any system which comes into contact with it.) |
| (1) The teachings of Hinduism stress Universal toleration and acceptance of all religions as true. Another outstanding characteristic of Hindu thought is its understanding of the nature of man and his relations with other beings in the universe. | Shushil K. Maitra, The Ethics of the Hindus, Calcutta: University of Calcutta, 1925. Poola T. Raju, Idealistic Thought of India, Cambridge: Harvard University Press, 1953. Rudolf Otto, Mysticism: East and West, New York: The Macmillan Co., 1932. |

| Study Outline | Notes and Sources |
|---|---|
| It stresses basic values like synthesis, desire to know the truth, and non-injury (ahimsa). | (Indian thought takes into its fold all nature. It is the harmony of man and nature.) (Hindu culture is comprehensive and suits the needs of every one, irrespective of caste, creed, color or sex.) |
| (2) Buddhism and Jainism preached the ethic of compassion. They believed that one can secure happiness by one's own ethical and intellectual efforts. | (Buddhism and Jainism originated in the sixth century B.C. Buddhism crossed the boundaries of India to Ceylon, Laos, Java, Borneo, Burma, Siam, and Cambodia, and then spread to Nepal, Tibet, Mongolia, Korea, China, Japan, Indonesia, etc.) |
| (3) Buddhism laid emphasis on the "four noble truths," viz. (i) Everything is misery and everything is imperfect; (ii) Desire is the root cause of this misery and this suffering; (iii) To escape from the eternal wheel of the Karma, i.e., one's doings, desire must be curbed, for only then can man find peace; (iv) This desire can be curbed by following the right | E. A. Burtt (ed.), The Teachings of the Compassionate Buddha, New York: The New American Library, 1955. |

| *Study Outline* | *Notes and Sources* |
|---|---|

path, i.e., Eightfold Path of
Buddha.

(4) Hinduism, Buddhism and Jainism
stressed civic responsibility,
social efficiency and happiness.

S. Radhakrishnan and Charles A.
Moore, A Source Book in Indian
Philosophy, New Jersey:  Princeton
University Press, 1957.

Nathmal Tatia, Studies in Jaina
Philosophy, Banaras, India:  Jain
Cultural Research Society, 1951.

(5) Vedanta influenced a series of
German thinkers from Fichte to
Schopenhauer and Deussen.

Arthur B. Keith, The Religion and
Philosophy of the Veda & Upanisads,
Harvard Oriental Series, 1925.

(6) Mahatma Gandhi, champion of non-
violence or ahimsa, influenced
the world with his teachings.

D. MacKenzie Brown, The White
Umbrella-Indian Political Thought
from Manu to Gandhi, Berkeley,
California:  University of California
Press, 1953.

(7) Today, the philosophies from
India are influencing the people
of the western hemisphere in
their approach to self-
understanding, the meaning of
personal freedom and relationship with other living beings.

S. K. Saksena, Nature of Consciousness
in Hindu Philosophy, Banaras, India:
Nand Kishore and Bros., 1944.

Filmer S. C. Northrop, The Meeting
of East & West, an Inquiry Concerning
World Understanding, New York:  The
Macmillan Co., 1946.

h)  India had a long tradition in the
arts and literature.

Surendra N. Dasgupta and S. K. De,
History of Sanskrit Literature,

| Study Outline | Notes and Sources |
|---|---|
| | Calcutta, University of Calcutta, 1947. |
| | John N. Farquhar, An Outline of the Religious Literature of India, London: Oxford University Press, 1920. |
| (1) The Vedic literature of the Aryans is the oldest Indian literature (1500 to 1000 B.C.). | A. Kaegi, The Rig Veda: The Oldest Literature of the Indians, Boston: Ginn & Co., 1886. (Veda means knowledge. Vedic literature consists of the four Vedas, the Brahmanas, the Aranyakas and the Upanishads.) |
| (2) The India of the Epics may be dated from 1000 B.C. to 500 B.C. This period produced two great Epic poems: Ramayana and Mahabharata. | Edward W. Hopkins, The Great Epic of India, New Haven: Yale University Press, 1928. (The epic poem Mahabharata describes the great war between the five sons of Pandu and the 100 sons of Dhritarastra, brother of Pandu. The epic poem Ramayana relates the expulsion of prince Rama and his wife Sita from Ayodhya, their wanderings in the forest, Sita's abduction by Ravana, the siege of Lanka (the present day Ceylon) and destruction of Ravana, and the triumphant return of the reunited couple to Ayodhya, |

| *Study Outline* | *Notes and Sources* |
|---|---|
| | their kingdom.) |
| (3) The Gita, perhaps a late addition to Mahabharata, teaches a religion of moral duty. | Swami Nikhilananda, The Bhagavad Gita (The Lord's Song), New York: Ramakrishna-Viveka nanda Center, 1944. |
| (4) Some of the Sanskrit works of the period (200 B.C. to 200 A.D.) were: The Laws of Manu, Natyasastra of Bharata, Patanjali's Mahabhasya, Asvaghosa's Buddhacarita, Sundarananda Kavya and Sariputra-Prakarana, and many others. | Pandurang V. Kane, History of Dharmasastra (Ancient and Medieval Religions and Civil Law in India), Bombay: Bhandarkar Oriental Research Institute, 1930-1953, 4 vols. |
| (5) In the fifth century A.D. the Kalidasa, "the Indian Shakespeare," flourished along with Dandin and Bharavi in the sixth century. | (Kalidasa's drama Sakuntala was first translated into English by Sir William Jones in the late 18th century and has ever since been recognized as a masterpiece by the non-Indian world. Kalidasa has written three Kavyas and three dramas.) |
| (6) In the domain of arts, India attained a high degree of development, viz. the caves of Ajanta and Ellora. | (Many of the paintings in Ajanta frescoes have disappeared, but what little remains shows a highly developed taste and deep aesthetic feeling.) |

(7) In the field of sculpture, the sculptors illustrated the stories on the walls of the temples. The images of the Buddha found at Sarnath are known for their serenity of expressions. The iron pillar (about 400 A.D.) near Delhi is an outstanding example of Indian craftmanship.

(The height of the iron pillar is 23 feet and 8 inches. The iron pillar is of a quality unknown to iron smelters until recent times.)

(8) Some of the outstanding wonders of India are, Juma Masjid, the Diwan-i-am and the Diwan-i-Khas, all in Delhi, and the Taj Mahal and Moti Masjid are the most prominent at Agra. The other memorable building of Bijapur is Gol Gumbuz with its unique "whispering gallery." This is one of the architectural wonders of the world.

(Distinct schools of architecture developed in India. Some of the examples are, Nagara style, vigorous style of the Sun Temple at Konarak, Indo-Aryan style at Khajuraho, Central India, Hoysala school, Vijayanagar style, etc. Mughal architecture was an amalgam of influences of Persia, Byzantium and India.)

(9) There was a well established musical tradition in India.

 (a) Sharangadeva of the 13th century A.D. wrote a book, Sangeetaratnakara, giving a

| Study Outline | Notes and Sources |
|---|---|

clear picture of Indian
achievement in the field of
music.

   (b) Music entered a new phase
      with the advent of Islam in
      India.

(Balban and Raziya were great patrons of music. Amir Khusru was an authority on the music of his time. Khayal, a style of Hindustani music, Drupad style of Hindustani music, Qawali, Thumri and Gazal became popular in India due to Muslim singers.)

   (c) In South India, Karnataka
      music was evolved. Vidyaranya
      is believed to be the origin-
      ator of this school. He wrote
      Sangitaratna, the first work
      on Karnataka or Dakshinadi
      music.

(Others like Rama Amatya and Purandara Dasa contributed to its development. The music of South India was also influenced by Islam.)

  i) There were traditional dance forms
    of several kinds.

    (1) Dancing as an art developed and
       then degenerated in North India.

    (2) In the south, the classical
       dance, Bharatanatya, flourished.

B.  The history of the East Indian immi-
    grants in the United States is a part

of their cultural heritage, and is
evidence of their own American identity.

1.  When they first arrived, few had
    thought of remaining permanently
    in the United States.  Most of
    them saw the U.S. as a land of
    economic opportunity which would
    provide them the means of gaining
    the security of land ownership
    and a measure of status when they
    returned home.

2.  Several factors influenced the immi-
    gration of East Indians to settle
    in North America.

    a)  Economic opportunities, publi-
        cized by steamship and industrial
        concerns brought many East Indians
        to America.

    b)  Many wanted to escape from famine
        and high taxation in India and
        thus came to America.

    c)  Political discontent at home drove
        many to North America.

    d)  They came to America to escape the
        low standard of living for

Rajani Kanta Das, Hindustani Workers
on the Pacific Coast, Berlin:  Walter
de Gruyter and Company, 1923.
(They did not become farmers, but for
the most part, earned wages in
mills, mines and factories.  After
earning enough money they intended
to return to their family and community in India.)

themselves and their families

which resulted from overpopulation.

e) East Indian immigration to the United States began in the middle of the nineteenth century. There were only two East Indians in the United States in 1859, five in 1860, six in 1861; but by 1910, 5409 and in 1915, the number of East Indians in California alone was about 7000.

f) The Immigration Act of 1917 restricted the immigration of laborers from India to the United States.

g) By 1924, immigration from India was completely stopped.

h) Only after, 1946, were East Indians allowed to immigrate to the U.S. The Act of 1965 completely rescinded the immigration restrictions for East Indians.

i) Now, there are a large number of East Indian Americans working in all walks of life. Most of them are professionals, viz. teachers,

R. G. 85, Roll No. 1, File No. 52903/110/1913-14 of the U.S. Dept. of Labor, Bureau of Immigration, Washington. Following are some statistics about the entry of East Indians to the United States from as early as 1881.

| Years | Number Entered |
|---|---|
| 1881-1890 | 260 |
| 1891-1900 | 68 |
| 1901-1910 | 4713 |
| 1911-1920 | 2082 |
| 1921-1930 | 1886 |
| 1931-1940 | 496 |
| 1941-1950 | 1761 |
| 1951-1960 | 1973 |
| 1961-1965 | 2602 |
| 1965 | 582 |
| 1966 | 2458 |
| 1967 | 4642 |
| 1968 | 4682 |
| 1969 | 5963 |
| 1970 | 10114 |
| 1971 | 14310 |

| *Study Outline* | *Notes and Sources* |
|---|---|
| doctors, professors, engineers, mathematicians, scientists, etc. | 1972    16926 |
|  | 1973    13124 |
|  | 1974    12779 |

Source:  Who's Who Among Indian Immigrants in North America
Directory, 1975.

3.  The East Indian family patterns and traditions influenced (and are still influencing) the home life of people from the Indian sub-continent.

Leo Davids, "The East Indian Family Overseas," Social and Economic Studies, Vol. 13, No. 3 (September 1964), 383-396.

a)  The early immigrants who came to America had to marry non-Indians. Absence of women of their ethnicity was an important condition prior to 1947.

Yusuf Dadabhay, "Circuitous Assimilation Among Rural Hindustanis in California," Social Forces, Vol. 33, No. 2 (December 1954), 138-141.
(By 1920, a few Indians had taken mainly Mexican-American wives. There were some who had married caucasians.)

b)  At first, marriages were arranged by parents for their sons and daughters.

(Marriage is still done by parental arrangement because a match with an Indian family cannot be handled directly by the prospective spouse.)

c)  The few "love matches" (love western style) usually are an active rebellion by American

(There appears to be a strong preference on the part of East Indian men for women from India.)

84

born young people. (Some India-
born young people do marry non-
Indians.)

d) The East Indian families prefer
sons because sons are instrumental in the salvation of their
parents after death.

e) The family was the center of all
activities--friendships, employment, marriage and organization.
When East Indians were discriminated against in employment due
to resistance from labor unions,
they went into farming or business
for themselves. Family members
and relatives were given preference in employment; again, family
enterprise was the pattern.

f) Discriminatory Laws did not permit
statutory quota for East Indian
women, which in turn, had dele-
terious effects upon East Indians
for many years.

(1) Many of them had married in
India and a few had children
but they had left their families

Milton Singer and Bernard S. Cohn,
Structure and Change in Indian
Society, Chicago: Aldine Publishing
Co., 1968.

W. E. Moore, Social Change, Englewood
Cliffs, New Jersey: Prentice-Hall,
Inc., 1963, 102-103.

(It seems that the East Indian family
has become increasingly similar to
the standard norms of American society,
or is moving towards the urbanized-
industrialized family pattern.)

| *Study Outline* | *Notes and Sources* |
|---|---|

when they came to the United
States. This situation created
intense emotional conflicts in
the lives of the East Indian
immigrants.

(2) As late as 1940, the ratio of
men to women was 5 :1. Absence
of women of East Indian origin
was an important condition
prior to 1947. Those East Indians who wanted to stay in
America could choose between
celibacy and intermarriage with
other ethnic groups.

Rajani Kant Das, Hindustani Workers
on the Pacific Coast, p. 109.

(3) Many East Indian men had to take
Mexican-American wives to provide some of the needs which
would ordinarily be met in a
family.

Yusuf Dadabhay, "Circuitous Assimilation Among Rural Hindustanis in
California," pp. 138-141.
(It should be remembered that for
sometime California legislation pro-
hibited marriages between Asians
and whites. Since before 1946,
peoples and races indigenous to
India were ineligible for naturalization; Hindustanis with wives in
India were prevented from bringing
their families to the United States.)

86

|                                    |                                    |
|------------------------------------|------------------------------------|
| <u>*Study Outline*</u>             | <u>*Notes and Sources*</u>         |

g) The East Indian immigrants who came after 1947, had a normal family life because they brought their families with them to America.

(1) Second and third generation East Indian, Pakistani and Bangla Deshi Americans preoccupied themselves with education and entering the professions.

(2) After the Second World War, a large number of scholars, students, businessmen and professionals from Indian sub-continent came to the United States though most Indians were not allowed to immigrate. Many of them brought their families with them to America.

(3) After 1965, the number of professionals emigrated from India to the United States with their families again increased. The entry of professionals from India is increasing every year.

(See the Immigration and Naturalization Act of 1965. Since these professionals have higher education and training they occupy responsible and wellpaying positions in academic institutions and industry.)

(4) With professional training and

87

education to match or surpass
any other group, they have removed themselves from employment such as their first American
forebearers found--laborers and
railroad builders.

(5) The East Indian way of life
(especially toleration, accom-
modation and docility) has made
cultural assimilation much
easier in the American society.

(6) Most of them have middle class
value system of middle class
America.

Kananur V. Chandra, Adjustment &
Attitudes of East Indian Students
in Canada, California:  R & E Research Associates, Inc., 1974.

(7) The American-born East Indian
Americans consider themselves
Americans, and, while they may
yet cling to certain aspects of
East Indian culture, they have
adopted many of the American
ways.

(8) Present-day East Indian, Pakistani and Bangla Deshi Americans
are interested in reviving their
ancient cultural heritage.

(They want to rediscover and safeguard
their own identity by going back to
their history and civilization to find
their roots and sustenance.)

h) Americans held stereotyped images of East Indian, Pakistani and Bangla Deshi Americans in the U.S. and thus reacted to them on the basis of those stereotypes. These reactions varied from group to group and had varying psychological effects toward the East Indian, Pakistani and Bangla Deshi groups.

1) There were positive perceptions.

(a) Some employers viewed them as the most desirable employees.

(1) These people were very hard workers and possessed a strong sense of duty.

(2) The new immigrants were often willing to work at lower wages than other groups.

(3) They were instrumental in reclaiming and developing various spacious plantations and land.

(The immigrants who came to America proved themselves to be hard workers, not requiring supervision. The work ethic of East Indians was comparable to that of Protestant work ethic.)

(b) The East Indian culture, which was reflected in community and family life, fits in very

well with American social in-

stitutions.

(1) Family is an important in-

    stitution and bears the re-

    sponsibility of rearing and

    acculturation of the young

    into the larger society.

(2) The East Indian children be-

    haved well and respected

    elders and authority.

(3) Most of the families were

    patriarchal but the role of

    the mother was very impor-

    tant in maintaining sta-

    bility at home.

(4) The East Indians brought         Rajendra Prasad, At the Feet of

    with them a tolerance for        Mahatma Gandhi, New York:  Philo-

    other beliefs and ideas.         sophical Library, 1955.

(5) Most of them brought with        S. Radhakrishnan, The Hindu View of

    them a strong sense of ob-       Life, London:  George Allen & Unwin,

    ligation to the community        Ltd., 1927.

    as well as to the family.

(6) Most of them had high aspi-

    rations for social and

    economic status in American

society though such aspira-

tions often led to conflicts

with the host society.

2) There were negative views of the East Indians' competitiveness: American stereotypes were often highly unfavorable.

Jogesh C. Misrow, East Indian Immigration on the Pacific Coast, San Francisco, California: R & E Research Associates, 1971, reprint.

 a) American labor organizations considered East Indians as a threat.

 (1) Willingness to work during strike periods created a conviction among labor leaders that they were brought in to lower the scale of wages and to cripple the labor unions.

 (2) East Indians' willingness to work long hours for low wages was a threat to the security of other workers.

 (3) During the periods of economic difficulties, East Indians were used as scapegoats to blame for the hardships.

Jogesh C. Misrow, East Indian Immigration on the Pacific Coast, pp. 11-29.

91

b)  Negative stereotypes developed.

   (1) Jogesh Misrow and Chandra list the following as East Indian stereotypes in America: coolie laborer, Hindu mystic, turbaned Hindu, starving Indian, unassertive Indian, unassimilable foreigner, uncommunicable Indian.

   (2) East Indians inherited a number of the stereotypes associated with Chinese and Japanese.

   (3) News media and books were used to exploit the negative stereotypes and fears which had been the center of many a political campaigns.

(Even today news media and movies present the negative stereotypes of East Indian, Pakistani and Bangla Deshi Americans.)

(Macon Telegraph, a newspaper in Georgia reported on September 12, 1976, that during Christmas 1975, a midwestern city ran a Hindu sect out of town because it was not Christian.)

C.  Many East Indian, Pakistani and Bangla Deshi Americans have made outstanding contributions to their country and to the world in all fields of human achievement.

1. Today, they are to be found in every facet of human endeavor: teaching, research, engineering, mathematics, medicine, science and other professions.

2. The 1965 Immigration Act paved the way for East Indian professionals to come as immigrants to the United States. More than 95% of the immigrants are highly qualified with at least a university degree in some profession.

3. Dr. H. Govind Khorana, Professor and Co-Director of Institute of Enzyme Research, University of Wisconsin, was awarded the 1968 Nobel Prize for breaking the genetic code.

4. Dr. Subramanyan Chandrasekhar, Professor of Astro-Physics, Enrico-fermi Institute, Chicago, is a world renouned scientist.

5. Dr. Rama Murthy, Researcher at Massachusetts Institute of Technology, has recombined the genetic material.

6. A large number of East Indian, Pakistani and Bangla Deshi Americans are engaged in teaching and research on university faculties throughout the United States.

7. Mr. Zubin Mehta, Music Conductor, is well known in America.

8. Additional research will acquaint the student with many more outstanding contributors.

D. During and after Second World War,
   many Americans had traveled in Asia
   and thus developed an understanding
   of immigrants who had come or were
   coming from the Indian sub-continent
   as students and suppliers of needed
   scientific and technological skills.

   1. Recent United States economic and

technical assistance programs have

brought an increasing number of

students and trainees from the sub-

continent for education and higher

technical training.

2.  American educators, economists,

    scientists and the public have

    gained a first-hand knowledge of

    Indian peoples from the sub-

    continent.  After visiting the

    Asian countries including India,

    they have returned with increased

    respect and admiration for Indian

    cultures and for the people.

3.  Today, the philosophies from India          Newsweek, September 6, 1976, pp. 56-62.

    are influencing the people of the

    Western Hemisphere in their approach

    to self-understanding, the meaning

    of personal freedom and relation-

    ships with other living beings.

4.  The cultural imprint of East In-             (There are Yoga temples, Trans-

    dians in various parts of North             cendental meditation centers, and

    America is not difficult to dis-            yogic research institutes.  Many

    cover.                                      schools, colleges and universities

                                               have introduced courses in yoga,

Indian philosophies and religions,

and transcendental meditation.)

PART II: EAST INDIAN, PAKISTANI AND BANGLA
DESHI AMERICANS' CONFLICT

I. Introduction

The East Indian Americans were classified as non-Anglo-Saxons. They were readily identifiable as Asians because of their dress, religion, food habits and choice of entertainment. They became a _arget of organized labor and dishonest politicians who were exploiting the masses by using East Indians as scapegoats.

The reactions of the East Indian Americans varied. Some of the immigrants who experienced discrimination became touchy and avoided contacts with white Americans. Others removed themselves from the scene of greatest conflict. Whenever they were subjected to discriminatory laws they grouped together for protection.

To circumvent the discriminatory practices, East Indians became more efficient than the whites in business, farming and education.

II. Guide and Sourcebook

| *Study Outline* | *Notes and Sources* |
|---|---|
| A. People from the Indian sub-continent emigrated to the shores of America where they thought to find means to better conditions for their families due to many conflicts--both internal and external--in their country of origin. | C. Kondapi, Indians Overseas: 1838-1949. (Kondapi presents a detailed account of the Indian emigration and the main reasons for the immigration to the United States and other countries of the world--to seek economic opportunities, to seek an easier and richer livelihood, working for money away from home and colonizing among English speaking white people. |
| 1. Early Indian emigration was largely cultural and commercial. | R. C. Majumdar, Ancient Indian Colonies in the Far East, Vol. I, Champa. |
| 2. Indian economy could not escape the effects of the Industrial Revolution | L. C. Knowles, Economic Development of the Overseas Empire, Vol. I. |

96

| Study Outline | Notes and Sources |
|---|---|

in the West which, in turn, destroyed
the indigenous handicraft industries.

3. To add to all these, caste exclu-
siveness and prejudice prevented
people from entering occupations
other than those allowed by caste
and custom.

Sir John Strachey, India, Its Administration and Progress, The Report of
the Famine Commission, 1880, Vol. I.

4. There was a great demand for plan-
tation and agricultural labor in
Hawaii and the mainland United
States.

5. East Indian and Pakistani students
and intellectuals who came for education and higher training chose to
make America their home because of
rapid growth in numbers of educated
unemployed back home.

The Asian Student, San Francisco,
California, March 30, 1963.

6. For many, education in the United
States was a device to escape home
and find better opportunities
abroad.

William H. Strain, "Some Doubts
about Educational Exchange," College
and University, Vol. 42, No. 2
(Winter, 1967), 141-146.

7. Scientists, engineers and medical
professionals reluctantly left the
sub-continent for America in search
of a promised land.

Usha Paranjpe, "The Foreign Trained
Student of Asia," The Asian Student,
May 19, 1959.

B. Early Indian immigrants to the Pacific

Coast of North America were steamship
crews, soldiers, workers and students.

1.  The Indo-European and several
    British steamship companies used
    to employ East Indian crews.  In
    the course of their voyages, when
    the ships touched American shores,
    they liked the country, its oppor-
    tunities and its people, and they
    decided to adopt it as their new
    home.

Jogesh C. Misrow, East Indian Immi-
gration on the Pacific Coast, San
Francisco, California:  R&E Research
Associates, 1971.

2.  After 1893, Indian students began
    to come to American universities
    and some of them decided to stay on.

3.  During the Boxer up-rising in
    China, East Indian workers and
    soldiers who were in China came in
    contact with the soldiers both of
    the United States and Canada.
    After the trouble was over, a large
    number of them migrated to the
    United States and Canada instead of
    going back to India.

Chirol, The Unrest in India.

C.  On their arrival in America East
    Indian immigrants were subject to
    overt and covert discrimination in

Also see Part I.

| Study Outline | Notes and Sources |
|---|---|

all walks of life.  East Indians,
like the Chinese in America, were the
scapegoats in economic struggles.

1. The first official record of the
   arrival of the East Indians in the
   United States was registered in
   1859.

2. American politicians who believed
   in Nordic ethnocentricism insti-
   gated the white masses to drive
   East Indians back to India.

3. As a climax of the agitation against
   East Indian laborers, several bills
   were introduced in the Congress

*Notes and Sources column:*

Reports of the Immigration Commission,
Vol. I, Washington, 1911, p. 79.
Rajani Kant Das, Hindustan Workers
on the Pacific Coast, p. 3.
United States Immigration Commission
Reports, Hearings on Hindu Immigration, Part II, 1914, p. 105.
(The Commissioner General of Immigration in his annual reports wrote:
"The Hindu propaganda ... is calculated to give much trouble ... make
plans for the protection of the
country against the influx of aliens
who cannot be readily and health-
fully assimilated in our body politic.")
(By the term "Hindu Propaganda," the
Commissioner General refers to the
notion that if the laws are not strict
enough all India will rush to American
shores.)
Elizabeth S. Kite, The Modern Review
(February 1927), p. 169.

with provisions for the exclusion

of the East Indians from the United

States in 1913 and 1914.  These

bills proposed tu apply to the

East Indian all the provisions of

the Chinese Exclusion Act of 1882.

4.  The immigration officials began to

turn back East Indians who applied

for admission to the U.S. on false

pretenses such as liability to be-

come a public charge, inability to

earn a living, and/or having a

mental or physical defect.

5.  In the year 1910, a large number

of East Indians were turned back to

India at San Francisco on willful

misrepresentation of immigration

laws.

6.  On February 5, 1917, the United          (For a statement of the Indian case

States Congress passed the Natural-          see The Modern Review (June 1914),

ization Act and the Immigration              624-28.

Act (Barred Zone Immigration Act).

This act expressly excluded the

people from Asia in barred zones,

defined arbitrarily by certain

latitudes and longitudes, which

included the Indian sub-continent.

7. The Immigration Act of 1917 restricted labor immigration from
   India to the U.S. but it allowed
   a small number of students and
   businessmen under special visas.

8. The Act also gave much more power          Edward P. Hutchinson, "Immigration
   to immigration officials, required         Policy since World War II," in *Immi-*
   literacy tests for those over 16           *gration:  An American Dilemma* (ed.),
   years of age, and doubled the head-        Boston:  Benjamin Munziegler, 1953.
   tax.                                       (Actually, however, the literacy
                                              test was a deliberate attempt to
                                              limit the number of immigrants from
                                              Asia and give preference to Europeans.)

9. Those who had been permanently
   domiciled in the United States before May 1, 1917, had to obtain
   a reentry permit even though they
   allowed to depart temporarily for
   a short period.

10. The restrictive nature of the immi-       United States v. Thind, 261 U.S. 204
    gration legislation and practices,        (1922).
    as it concerned East Indians, was         (The Judge decided that East Indians
    reinforced by a decision on February      were not, in the opinion of the common
    19, 1923, in which Justice Suther-        man, Caucasians, whatever might be
    land of the Supreme Court of the          their race from a purely biological

United States held that a Hindu
was not a "white person" within the
meaning of the revised Statute
2169, relating to the naturalization of aliens, and hence ineligible for American citizenship.

11. The Judgement of the Supreme Court
disentitled East Indians to any
quota under the 1924 Immigration
Act.  It resulted in a virtual
cessation of immigration from
India.

12. The Supreme Court decision reaf-
firmed the policy of cancellation
of most citizenship certificates
of East Indians who had been
naturalized for a 15-year period
after 1908.

Harold S. Jacoby, "More Sinned
Against than Sinning," The Pacific
Historian, II (November 1958), pp.
1-8.

13. Some categories such as tourists,
students, visitors, etc. from
India might enter the United States
as non-quota immigrants but were
not eligible to U.S. citizenship.

(The immigration policy of the
United States was not one of selection
or regulation but of exclusion of
East Indians mostly on racial grounds,
though the U.S. Government advanced
economic reasons.)

14. Some still entered illegally.
Jacoby makes a conservative estimate

viewpoint.)

Jacoby, A Half Century Appraisal of
East Indians, p. 1.

that as many as 3000 East Indians
entered the U.S. between 1920 and
1930.

D.  A long series of discriminatory laws
were imposed upon East Indians to
restrict their opportunities.

  1.  Bills were introduced to exclude      H. Brett Melendy, The Oriental
      Asians from schools attended by       Americans, New York:  Twayne Pub-
      white children, to prevent aliens     lishers, Inc., 1972.
      from becoming members of boards of
      directors of California corpora-
      tions, and to permit municipalities
      to segregate into specified areas
      those "aliens whose presence may be
      inimical to health and public
      morals."

  2.  There were two anti-alien land        John W. Caughey, California, Englewood
      laws passed in California in 1913      Cliffs, 1953, 470-471.
      and in late 1920, the latter by
      initiative procedure.

  3.  While East Indian immigrants were     (On May 13, 1913, a California Alien
      unable to hold legal title to land,   Land Bill, was passed to provide that
      the non-Indian spouse had title to    aliens, i.e., Asians, might lease
      the land.                             land for a maximum of 3 years only,
                                            and not bequeath it.  The aim of this
                                            measure was to drive the Asians out

| *Study Outline* | *Notes and Sources* |
|---|---|

of rural areas.)

(The amended Alien Land Law in 1920, denied East Indians the right to own or lease land and the right to live in peace.)

E. Prejudice and discrimination against East Indians erupted into open hostility on the Pacific Coast

   1. Americans ridiculed East Indians as "Smoke-colored Orientals" and "colored, turnaned Hindus."

The New York Times, December 9, 1915, sec. 6, 1:1.

   2. There were riots in the city of Bellingham, Washington State, when several East Indian laborers, working in the sawmills were mobbed by white men. For fear of bodily injury, East Indians left the community.

(An American newspaper reporter narrates the plight of an East Indian scholar who came to visit North America to study the educational systems of Canada and the United States, and was pelted by white mobs.)

   3. Labor organizations denied membership to East Indian laborers.

   4. Violent demonstrations by the Asiatic Exclusion League were made in San Francisco against oriental immigration. It was specifically directed against the East Indian Sikhs who wore turbans in America.

Pacific Monthly, Vol. 7, 1905, p. 584.

F. With the demand for laborers in agri-
culture and industry, East Indians
came to America in greater numbers.

  1. In the beginning, East Indians on
the Pacific Coast were all men and
generally came with the intention
of earning money and going back to
India.

  2. They worked in different industries
and manufacturing establishments in
Washington State, Oregon and
California.

  3. Eventually, many entered the field
of agricultural industries as this
was their occupation in India.

  4. They developed Twitchel Island in
California and various spacious
plantations in other parts of the
country.

  5. East Indians worked in celery
fields, citrus orchards, beet
fields, the raisin industry, the
California wine industry, and
other related agricultural fields.

G. There were economic and ethnic reasons
for the fears of the American white

(Most of them went back to India
after spending several years in the
U.S. but a small number of them decided to stay.)

U.S. Immigration Commission Reports,
The Hearings on the Hindu Immigration,
Part I, 1914, p. 68.

community toward the East Indian
presence.  The argument that the
standard of living of the people
would go down due to the Asian
presence was false.  Excessive laws
and other measures to curb the Asian
immigration were unjustified and
discriminative.

1.  The new comer, despite his initia-
    tive and vigor, began at the bottom
    of the social ladder.

2.  The American government kept Indian
    women out on purpose, intending to
    force the Hindi to return home in-
    stead of settling permanently.

3.  East Indians were used as strike-
    breakers by employers.  This cre-
    ated animosity and anger among the
    strikers.

4.  Many East Indian laborers who came
    to the Pacific Coast did not want
    to work as laborers for long.
    Many, perhaps most, wanted to own
    and work their own land.  A majority
    of whites did not like the ambitions

Leo Davids, "The East Indian Family
Overseas," Social and Economic Studies,
Vol. 13, No. 3 (September 1964), p. 388.
(The turban and beard were shed very
quickly due to their high visibility.)
Elizabeth Kite, Modern Review.

of these workers.

5. The frugality of East Indians became a sore point with whites who
envied their ability for "upward
mobility."

6. The prejudice was partly an un-
reasoned color phobia, based on
fear and hate and partly due to
a dislike of the East Indian dress,
religion, and manner of living.

H. The East Indian reaction was mild in
the face of hostility due to several
important factors.

1. The Indian government was not interested in the fate of its citizens because:

a) India was a colony of Britain and
the natives were considered as
colored people.

b) Britain was interested in maintaining good relationship with
the Canadian and American governments.

(The Canadian authorities made the
proposal to American authorities that
they should exclude East Indians as
they had excluded the Chinese.)

c) The policy of exclusion of East
Indians originated through British
initiative.

| *Study Outline* | *Notes and Sources* |
|---|---|
| 2. East Indians in agriculture co-operated among themselves by lending money without interest or with a very low interest rate, and, parenthetically, without legal record. | Lawrence A. Wenzel, "The Rural Punjabis of California: A Religio-Ethnic Group," Phylon, Vol. 2, (Fall, 1968), 252. |
| 3. These workers organized their own groups to safeguard the interests of their people. The duties of the elected officials in the group were to explore new opportunities of employment, to disseminate information on working conditions, wages, and other related matters. | (Cooperation was the basic principle of the organizations of the East Indians in the United States.) |
| 4. Religion played a large part in the lives of East Indians in America. The element of self-restraint further served to enrich the immigrants' personality. At the same time, they knew that they were outnumbered by the white people | (In some cases, for fear of bodily injury, East Indians left the community.) |
| 5. If he was denied a job in the white society he opened his own retail business or worked on his own land and became self-dependent. | |

| *Study Outline* | *Notes and Sources* |
|---|---|

6. If they were denied justice in American courts they set up their own organizations to settle their disputes.

Rajani Kant Das, Hindustani Workers on the Pacific Coast, Berlin, 1923, p. 66.

7. The East Indian laborers segregated themselves in some areas due to white restrictions on residential areas. White restrictions were a factor in creating these segregated East Indian communities.

I. Conditions encountered by the early East Indian community led to personal or group conflicts.

1. The immigration laws separated families from their loved ones creating emotional conflicts among the members.

Leo Davids, "The East Indian Family Overseas," pp. 383-96.
(The laborers could not, until after the Second World War, bring wives from India. The American and Canadian governments kept Indian women out on purpose, intending to force East Indian men to return home instead of settling permanently.)

J. Only after the Second World War, Americans have begun to right the wrongs committed against Asian Americans:

C. Kondapi, Indians Overseas: 1838-1949, p. 434.
(During the hearings before the U.S. Congress on Emanuel Celler's Bill to

| Study Outline | Notes and Sources |
|---|---|

1.  The Luce-Celler Bill was passed by both Houses of Congress and received the President's assent on July 2, 1946.

give a quota to East Indians, many witnesses claimed that it would eliminate racial discrimination against East Indians and every witness who opposed racial discrimination supported the quota system which would permit about 100 Indians to enter the United States every year. But actually the quota law was only another name for racial discrimination.)

2.  This law also removed India from the Barred Zone, thus allowing India to be assigned a quota set at 100 per year. Even this little trickle of new immigrants had to satisfy the personal tests stipulated by the immigration regulations relating to literacy, freedom from disease, financial solvency, etc.

3.  In 1950 Congressman Walter H. Judd introduced a measure to authorize the naturalization of any qualified alien without respect to race or national origin.

Lynn P. Dunn, Asian Americans, California: R&E Research Associates, 1975, p. 84.

(President Truman vetoed the immigration Bill.)

4.  The Walter-McCarran Immigration and
    Naturalization Act of 1952 was
    passed and the immigration quotas
    continued to be heavily weighted
    in favor of North Europeans.

5.  The enactment of the Immigration
    and Naturalization Act of 1965, re-
    laxed the immigration restrictions
    of East Indians by abolishing the
    quota system.  This bill was signed
    by President Lyndon B. Johnson in
    1965.

Thomas L. Bernard, "United States
Immigration Laws and the Brain Drain,"
*International Migrations*, Vol. 7,
Nos. 3, 4, 1969, pp. 31-38.
(The passage of this important Act
contained provisions for a two and a
half year transitional period before
becoming fully effective on July 1,
1968.
This Act is of particular significance
in that it marked the abandonment of
the traditional and controversial
quota system based on the discriminatory criterion of national origins.
The new system is no less controversial, but for different reasons,
as was expressed by the Vice-President
of the United States Walter Mondale
who feels that "the national origins
quota system was a shameful form of
discrimination.  We place high value

on the free movement of individuals
between nations ... especially if
we need their talent and skills.")
Walter Mondale, University of Minnesota, Proceedings of the Conference
on Higher Education and the International Flow of Manpower, Minneapolis, Minnesota, April 1967, p. 84.

PART III: INTEGRATION VERSUS NATIONALISM
EAST INDIAN, PAKISTANI AND BANGLA DESHI AMERICANS' DILEMMA

I.  Introduction

Most American immigrants from the Indian sub-continent had strong nationalistic feelings.  They maintained tenaciously cultural and family ties with the
old country, supporting their families (parents, wives, children, brothers and
sisters) in the sub-continent.  The early immigrants hoped to return to India
for retirement with family and relatives.

The restrictive laws in the United States strengthened the cultural ties to
the land of birth and intensified nationalistic feelings.

The second and third generation American-born children of the East Indians
consider themselves American, and, while they may yet cling to certain aspects
of East Indian culture, they tend to speak American English and they have successfully adopted many of the American ways.  They want complete integration and
cultural assimilation into the American society.

The present status of East Indian Americans lies somewhere between the poles
of nationalism and integration.  Most of them have fully internalized the middle
class cultural values of America.

II.  Guide and Sourcebook

| *Study Outline* | *Notes and Sources* |
|---|---|
| A. Early East Indian Americans held tenaciously to their cultural identity and to the hope of return to India for reunion with family and extended relatives. | Lawrence A. Wenzel, "The Rural Punjabis of California:  A Religio-Ethnic Group," Phylon, Vol. 29 (Fall 1968), pp. 245-256. |
| 1. Early East Indian Americans were united by a common cultural tradition in which the most noticeable characteristics were the philosophy and religion, language, food habits, dress, and a keen interest in Indian national affairs. | |

| *Study Outline* | *Notes and Sources* |
|---|---|
| 2. The language barrier was an incentive to the first East Indian immigrants to join together. | (Many East Indian Americans formed eating clubs and hired one of their own as professional cook.) |
| 3. Loyalty of these Americans to their families was reflected in their financial support of their families and relatives and social institutions such as schools, temples and monasteries in their villages. | |
| 4. Evidence of lose ties of East Indian Americans to the sub-continent of India is found in the fact that they wore the national or local Indian dress. | (Even today many immigrants from the Indian sub-continent wear their national costume in America.) |
| 5. The drawing of spouses from India is partly a necessity and partly a preference. | (The constant immigration keeps Indian culture alive, maintains the "preference quota" of families already in the United States, and perhaps brings in women who have the much desired East Indian cultural traits.) |
| 6. Periodically, East Indian Americans visit the Indian sub-continent to meet their relatives and friends. This retains their ties with the land of their ancestors. | |

114

B.  Discrimination and hostility by Cau-
    casian groups and the general immi-
    gration and legal controls imposed
    upon them intensified nationalistic
    feelings of East Indian Americans.

    1.  East Indian newspapers and maga-
        zines were also a part of East
        Indian American separatism.  (There
        were 13 East Indian publications in
        the United States in 1976.)

    2.  Leadership in the struggle for
        equal rights and equal justice
        developed among many East Indian
        American citizens.

    3.  Many East Indian Americans supported          L. P. Mathur, Indian Revolutionary
        the Indian revolutionaries against            Movement in the U.S.A., Delhi:  S.
        the British rule in India.                    Chand & Co., 1970.
                                                      (The support was possible because a
                                                      large number of Indian settlers were
                                                      already dissatisfied with the treat-
                                                      ment given to them in Canada and the
                                                      failure of the British government to
                                                      protect the interests of the East
                                                      Indian immigrants in North America.

C.  American-born children of East Indian
    Americans opposed the separatism of

their parents.  As American citizens
they wanted to be fully integrated
into the American society.

1.  The immigrants from the sub-continent
    have been law abiding citizens.  As
    a result, most of the children obey
    laws and try to become good citi-
    zens because it is a disgrace to
    the family for a child to be in
    trouble with the law.

2.  Young East Indian Americans have
    surpassed all groups in terms of
    number of years of school com-
    pleted.

D.  Unlike other militant minority groups          Newsweek, August 30, 1976, pp. 55-56.
    in the United States, viz., Black
    Power Movement and other Black Groups;
    Chicano Power Groups, East Indians
    did not receive the attention of the
    American public as to their problems
    of racial discrimination (both from
    White and Black Americans) in educa-
    tion, employment, housing and other
    related areas.  As a result, there
    has developed, in the last few years,
    a new East-Indian American

nationalism with Third World leanings.

## Conclusion

The history of the East Indian Americans in the United States covers a much shorter span of time than most of the other ethnic groups in America. They have been coming to the coterminous United States for less than a century. The span of their history in mainland U.S. is shorter than that of American Indians, Blacks, Chicanos, Chinese, Japanese, or Puerto Ricans.

Most of the East Indians had their own cultural identities to serve as bases on which to move into the American cultural mainstream.

Discrimination and hostility by American groups and the general immigration and legal controls imposed upon them intensified nationalism. But, their nationalism lacked the militancy of Black or Chicano militants.

Even today, pockets of intolerance against East Indians remain in America. The American-born sons and daughters of the East Indian immigrants have adopted many of the American ways. The young people dress like their white contemporaries, dance to the same music, attend the same schools and more or less pursue the same goals. They are fully acculturated, if not assimilated.

BIBLIOGRAPHY

Akhilananda, Swamy. Mental Health and Hindu Psychology. New York: Haper & Row, 1951.

Brown, D. M. The White Umprella-Indian Political Thought from Manu to Gandhi. Berkeley, California: University of California Press, 1953.

Burtt, E. A., ed. The Teachings of the Compassionate Buddha. New York: The New American Library, 1955.

Caughey, John W. California. Englewood Cliffs, 1953.

Chandra, Kananur V. Adjustment & Attitudes of East Indian Students in Canada. San Francisco, California: R&E Research Associates, Inc., 1974.

Chirol. The Unrest in India.

Das, Rajani Kant. Hindustani Workers on the Pacific Coast. Berlin: Walter de Gruyter and Company, 1923.

Dasgupta, Surendra N., and De, S. K. History of Sanskrit Literature. Calcutta, India: University of Calcutta, 1947.

Dunn, Lynn P. Asian Americans. San Francisco, California: R&E Research Associates, 1975.

Farquhar, John N. An Outline of the Religious Literature in India. London: Oxford University Press, 1920.

Hopkins, Edward W. The Great Epic of India. New Haven, Connecticut: Yale University Press, 1928.

Jacoby, Harold S. A Half Century Appraisal of East Indians.

Kaegi, A. The Rig Veda: The Oldest Literature of the Indians. Boston: Ginn & Co., 1886.

Kane, Pandurang V. History of Dharmasastra. (Ancient and Medieval Religious and Civil Law in India.) Bombay, India: Bhandarkar Oriental Research Institute, 1930-1953.

Keith, Arthur B. The Religion and Philosophy of the Veda and Upanisads. Harvard Oriental Series, 1925.

Knowles, L. C. Economic Development of the Overseas Empire. Vol. I.

Kondapi, C. Indians Overseas: 1838-1949. London: Oxford University Press, 1951.

Kramrisch, S. Indian Sculpture. London: 1937.

_____. The Art of India; Traditions of Indian Sculpture, Painting, & Architecture. 3rd ed. London: Phaidon Press, 1965.

Maitra, Shushil K. The Ethics of the Hindus. Calcutta, India: University of Calcutta, 1925.

Majumdar, R. C. Ancient Indian Colonies in the Far East. Vol. I. Champa.

_____. Hindu Colonies in the Far East. Calcutta, India: Firma K. L. Mukhopadhyay, 1963.

Masson-Oursel, Paul. Comparative Philosophy. New York: Harcourt, Brace & Co., 1926.

Mathur, L. P. Indian Revolutionary Movement in the U.S.A. Delhi, India: S. Chand & Co., 1970.

Melendy, H. Brett. The Oriental Americans. New York: Twayne Publishers, Inc., 1972.

Misrow, Jogesh C. East Indian Immigration on the Pacific Coast. San Francisco, California: R&E Research Associates, Inc., 1971.

Mondale, Walter. Proceedings of the Conference on Higher Education and the International Flow of Manpower. Minneapolis, Minnesota: University of Minnesota, 1967.

Moore, W. E. Social Change. Englewood Cliffs, New Jersey: Prentice-Hall, 1963.

Murthy, H. V. S., and Kamath, S. U. Studies in Indian Culture. New York: Asia Publishing House, 1973.

Nikhilananda, Swami. The Bhagavad Gita (The Lord's Song). New York: Ramakrishna-Vivekananda Center, 1944.

Northrop, Filmer S. C. The Meeting of East & West, an Inquiry Concerning World Understanding. New York: The Macmillan Co., 1946.

Otto, Rudolf. Mysticism: East and West. New York: The Macmillan Co., 1932.

Prasad, Rajendra. At the Feet of Mahatma Gandhi. New York: Philosophical Library, 1955.

Radhakrishnan, S., and Moore, Charles A. A Source Book in Indian Philosophy. New Jersey: Princeton University Press, 1957.

Radhakrishnan, S. The Hindu View of Life. London: George & Unwin, Ltd., 1927.

Raju, Poola T. Idealistic Thought of India. Cambridge, Massachusetts: Harvard University Press, 1953.

Reports of the Immigration Commission, Vol. I., Washington, 1911.

Saksena, S. K. Nature of Consciousness in Hindu Philosophy. Banaras, India: Nand Kishore and Bros., 1944.

Sarkar, Benoy K.  Hindu Achievement in Exact Sciences.  New York:  Longmans, Green & Co., 1918.

Shastra, Prabhu D.  The Essentials of Eastern Philosophy.  New York:  The Macmillan Co., 1928.

Singer, Milton, and Cohn, Bernard S.  Structure and Change in Indian Society.  Chicago, Illinois:  Aldine Publishing Co., 1968.

Spear, Percival.  India:  A Modern History.  Ann Arbor, Michigan:  The University of Michigan Press, 1961.

Tatia, Nathmal.  Studies in Jaina Philosophy.  Banaras, India:  Jain Cultural Research Society, 1951.

United States Immigration Commission Reports, Hearings on Hindu Immigration, Part II, 1914.


## Journals and Magazines


Bernard, Thomas L.  "United States Immigration Laws and the Brain Drain."  International Migrations, Vol. 7, Nos. 3, 4 (1969).

Dadabhay, Yusuf.  "Circuitous Assimilation Among Rural Hindustanis in California."  Social Forces, Vol. 33, No. 2 (December 1954).

Davids, Leo.  "The East Indian Family Overseas."  Social and Economic Studies, Vol. 13, No. 3 (September 1964).

Hutchinson, Edward P.  "Immigration Policy Since World War II."  Immigration:  An American Dilemma, ed.  Boston:  Benjamin Munziegler, 1953.

Jacoby, Harold S.  "More Sinned Against than Sinning."  The Pacific Historian, Vol. II (November 1958).

Kitte, Elizabeth S.  The Modern Review, February 1927.

Macon Telegraph, September 12, 1976.

Newsweek, August 30, 1976.

Newsweek, September 6, 1976.

The New York Times, December 9, 1915.

Paranjpe, Usha.  "The Foreign Trained Student of Asia."  The Asian Student, May 19, 1959.

Strain, William H.  "Some Doubts about Educational Exchange."  College and University, Vol. 42, No. 2 (Winter 1967).

The Asian Student, San Francisco, California, March 30, 1963.

Wenzel, Lawrence A.  "The Rural Punjabis of California:  A Religio-Ethnic Group."
    Phylon, Vol. 29 (Fall 1968).